Fifty
Shades
of Domination

Fifty Shades
of Domination

My True Story

MISTRESS MIRANDA

JOHN BLAKE

Published by John Blake Publishing Ltd,
3 Bramber Court, 2 Bramber Road,
London W14 9PB, England

www.johnblakepublishing.co.uk

www.facebook.com/Johnblakepub `facebook`
twitter.com/johnblakepub `twitter`

First published in paperback in 2014

ISBN: 978-1-78219-748-5

British Library Cataloguing-in-Publication Data:

A catalogue record for this book is available from the British Library.

Design by www.envydesign.co.uk

Printed in Great Britain by CPI Group (UK) Ltd

1 3 5 7 9 10 8 6 4 2

Papers used by John Blake Publishing are natural, recyclable products made
from wood grown in sustainable forests. The manufacturing processes conform
to the environmental regulations of the country of origin.

Every attempt has been made to contact the relevant copyright-holders, but some
were unobtainable. We would be grateful if the appropriate people could contact us.

CONTENTS

FOREWORD

Many families have secrets; the skeletons of long forgotten mistakes or indiscretions lurking in the cupboard for years, tucked away from the light and never to be spoken of again. In my case, my family had a secret which I only learnt through local gossip when I was nine-years-old.

I discovered at primary school that all of the family relationships I had ever known were one big lie. The two people I knew as my mum and dad weren't really my mum and dad at all – they were my grandparents. My real birth-mother had left home years before, leaving me behind and starting an entirely new family.

The revelation shattered my world. It turned out that the woman I thought was my big sister was really my mum, my nephew was really my brother, my niece was my baby sister and my elderly cousins were all aunts and uncles. My paternal grandparents had not wanted to know me, and my real dad was nowhere to be seen.

It was, in short, a confusing time all round.

There's a famous phrase of recent years, originally written by the poet Philip Larkin, which strikes a chord with me whenever I hear its somewhat crude sentiment: 'They fuck you up, your mum and dad.'

In my case, my parents didn't 'fuck up' my life, they merely confused it. They may even have done me a favour by helping mould me into a much-desired dominatrix and making me the strong, independent and successful businesswoman I like to believe I am today.

My worry, however, is how to tell the tale of how I grew up to be a star of the adult film world, and Britain's foremost dominatrix, without confusing any of you kind enough to read my story.

Until they day they died, I called my grandparents 'Mum and Dad', and knew my birth-mother simply by her first name. But for the sake of clarity, I shall refer throughout this narrative to my maternal grandparents – the couple who became my adoptive parents – as 'Nan' and 'Granddad' and I've given the title 'Mum' back to my birth-mother. (All other names, including relatives, friends, clients, partners, have been changed to protect anonymity.)

Confused? Quite probably! But please read on. All will, in due course, be explained.

– Miranda

CHAPTER 1

WELCOME TO MY WORLD

The lights had been dimmed in the business-class cabin of the United Airlines overnight flight from New York to London – the 'Red-Eye' as it is known to frequent travellers.

Most passengers were silent and still. Only a few were properly asleep but many had huddled down under their scarlet airline-issue blankets to try and snatch a few hours of fitful rest. My travelling companion in the adjacent seat, the wealthy sales director of a British computer company, was lying prone and also covered with a blanket. Neither he nor I, however, was expecting any sleep during the flight. I was awake because I am a professional dominatrix who was being paid to tease and hurt my neighbour mercilessly that night. He was most definitely not asleep because his hands were tied behind his back and regular jolts of electricity were coursing through the metal contacts of the elasticised

1

straps I'd wrapped tightly around his testicles and the glans of his penis.

I watched his face carefully as we lay, barely a foot apart, with just the shared armrest of the seat between us, our heads turned towards each other, and our eyes locked together in the dim light. Charles adores me looking deep into his eyes whilst I am torturing him, and years of experience have taught me that you can judge a man or woman's pain-endurance levels more accurately through their eyes than by any other method. The remote control device I was using, much like the one you use for your television, adjusts the strength of the battery-powered electric current rolling in waves across his genitalia. The trick is always to ensure that the discomfort levels are as high as my client can bear, without making him cry out in pain. The last thing Charles wanted was for one of the attentive stewardesses to notice anything amiss on their irregular patrols along the darkened aisle. I wouldn't really have minded if our kinky little game had been uncovered; I am often paid to humiliate my clients in public and was born with barely an embarrassment gene in my body. My only worry on this occasion was breaking the airline's rules against using 'an electronic device' in flight. They always claim, don't they, that it might interfere with the aircraft's navigation systems?

Glancing at one of the three watches habitually strapped to my wrist (yes, I know it's weird, but it's my own, private, time-keeping fetish) I realised that our fellow passengers would soon be stirring. It was time to bring our game to an end. I touched the remote control button one last time to ensure that Charles' penis and balls were suffering all the pain he desired. Then I made sure he was watching as I slipped a surgical-latex glove onto my hand. His excitement levels grew rapidly, his breath quickening and lips slightly parting, as my hand crept discreetly under the blanket draped across us. Fumbling in the darkness I squeezed the head of his cock, momentarily increasing the impact of the electrics and forcing the first, barely audible, moan of pain from deep in his throat. It was then but the work of a moment to rub my rubber-gloved fingers along his shaft and bring him to a shuddering sexual climax. My hand continued moving gently to give him as much afterglow pleasure as possible: a little reward for the pain he had endured. Honestly, I sometimes surprise myself with what a kind Mistress I can be! Then, still working by feel in the semi-darkness, I untied his hands, lay back in my seat and left him to clean himself up as best he could.

My *Emmanuelle*-type moment of teasing and torturing a client during a busy international flight is one of the more unusual requests I've fulfilled in nearly two decades as a professional dominatrix. The biggest challenge came not from playing the in-flight game but in carrying the equipment through airport security. The tiny battery pack and remote control easily pass as a phone or iPod, whilst the cock and ball straps have tiny metal contacts but look like a fashionable wrist-band. Neither had aroused any interest as we passed through Heathrow and Newark airports on the outward journey.

My aviation adventure was the climax, literally, of a three-day trip to the US as the paid companion of my London-based client, Charles, a regular visitor to my dungeon. He had planned it partly as a treat for me, but mostly because he was desperate to enliven an otherwise boring business trip that was of necessity keeping him away from his wife and his family. Staying together in a midtown Manhattan hotel, we had explored both the city and each other's BDSM (the acronym popularly employed as shorthand for Bondage, Domination, Sadism and Masochism) fantasies in a frantic day-and-night whirlwind of sightseeing and sexy games. It was far from being the first time that I had 'sessioned' with Charles, but we had never before had so much time together to tease out his deepest fantasies and fears.

For me there was the fascination of delving deep into Charles' mind and uncovering thoughts and desires that he had never openly admitted, even to himself. For him, there was the pleasure of my company by day and of the pain and torment I could bring him by night. The beauty of it was that Charles was not even, in a technical sense, being unfaithful to his wife. He, like all of the men who visit me, knows that I *never* have sex with my clients – well not with the male ones at least. A man may well receive some satisfaction at my hands, or at the mechanical hands of the intriguing variety of 'milking' and masturbation machines to be found in my dungeon, but sex with me is not on the menu.

The lack of penetration is rarely an issue with my visitors. They seek an experience which, whilst sexy and ultimately exciting, is centred more in their minds than in their testicles. For a complex variety of reasons they wish to be dominated, or controlled, or tightly bound in rubber or leather. They wish to be kinky and naughty and told off by a powerful and dominant woman. They wish to live out fantasies which may have haunted them from childhood. They long to test out their limits of pain, or suffocation or secret desires of bisexuality. In

4

short, they are seeking new experiences far removed from the 'vanilla' intercourse of their everyday lives.

My Manhattan-trip friend (many of my clients do go on to become friends) exhibited one trait which I have noticed over and over again in my years of intimately studying the male of our species. Returning to my side after each business meeting he was desperate to be mistreated and humiliated in every way possible. The more successful the business element of our trip became, the more urgent was his craving to be 'taken down a peg or two' by me. I have long known two truths about successful men: the more intelligent they are then the greater their desire for sexual adventure, and the more successful they are, the greater their need to be dominated. It is like the Chinese concept of yin and yang – a necessary balancing of their success with an equal measure of torment and despair. It does, thankfully, create a seemingly endless demand for me and for my fellow professional dominatrices around the world.

All in all, my American trip proved to be as successful as Charles' impressive sales' achievements: a substantial addition to my bank balance, some shop-till-you drop fun in New York, a couple of days sight-seeing as my client fulfilled his business obligations in the Big Apple, and an 'interesting' flight home. A not quite typical week in the life of Miss Miranda, aka 'The Bondage Mistress'.

Welcome to my world of professional domination.

CHAPTER 2

INTO THE
DUNGEON

I should like to say that my life consists of a succession of glamorous international flights, with a parade of charming and wealthy companions, but I'd be giving the wrong impression. True, there are enough rich men around to keep a girl happy and not short of a little luxury once in a while, but the deliciously perverted billionaires of *Fifty Shades of Grey* fame are somewhat short on the ground in the real world. There is, however, a constant supply of real men, real women and real couples who enjoy stretching their sexual boundaries by visiting a professional dominatrix. The publicity surrounding high-profile bondage-and-domination fans such as the former F1 motor-racing boss, Max Mosley, has combined with the success of the fictional, sadomasochistic, *Fifty Shades*-style erotica to stimulate interest in my previously secret world.

Once I would have preferred to stay in the shadows. I used to lie about what my job was by pretending to be a beauty therapist. Today, I can talk more freely of the secret pleasures I bring to many people. I can run a legitimate business, pay my taxes and enjoy the fruits of my labour as a businesswoman and entrepreneur. The sexual desires of others have brought me success and job satisfaction. Even so, the majority of my sexy games are played out, not in the mile-high-club surroundings of a Boeing 757, but in the more spacious and considerably better equipped surroundings of 'West London Towers' – my pet name for my warm and welcoming play premises.

Come with me now on a tour of that dungeon. I should perhaps say 'those dungeons' because here you'll find room after room of erotic and exotic equipment designed to stretch your senses and your body. You will, of course, only ever arrive at my door by appointment, perhaps from an initial and somewhat nervous telephone call or after an inquiring email to one of my websites. It used to be that I would answer every telephone inquiry myself, but with business so brisk, these days you may find yourself speaking with my professional answering service. A well-spoken young woman will discreetly ascertain that you wish to make an appointment with Miss Miranda before consulting my diary for an available date. It's an interesting sign of the times that my executive answering service has no more qualms about handling the affairs of a London dominatrix than it does about answering the calls of the businessmen and bankers who make up the bulk of their trade. On reflection… they probably consider that, compared with a banker, my adult-industry job makes *me* the more morally upright member of their clientele.

INTO THE DUNGEON

Whichever way you make initial contact, I will have asked for an email summarising your desires, with an outline of your sexual preferences and brief details of the particular services you require. The key word here is 'brief'. The emails I receive could form a book in themselves. A few will be concise and to the point: 'Rubber please – spanking and bondage – boot worship and breath control.' Others, despite my demand for brevity, run to pages of elaborate prose explaining scenarios of abduction, kidnap, interrogation and lengthy sentences of incarceration within the walls of my dungeon cells. For both of our sakes, I need to get inside your head before our session starts and understand your private fantasy needs. However, with the best will in the world, I rarely have time to read your 15 pages of erotica, eagerly describing every much-anticipated lash of my whip or detailing in boy-scout enthusiasm the precise knots you hope I will use to bind you to my bondage bench. We dominatrices call such behaviour 'topping from the bottom' – attempting to control every step of a session and leaving little room for our own cruel and creative contribution. I hate being constrained in that way because it removes all of the fun of my own input into our games. So, whether you are a lustful man or a curious woman, just place yourself, without reservation, into my not-so-tender hands and we'll both enjoy the experience so much more.

Entering my premises, you will be shown upstairs to the main dungeon and allowed a brief time alone to compose your thoughts and perhaps shower away the cares of your day. Here, your nervous excitement can build to the maximum. Around you sit the instruments of restriction, teasing and torment which may shortly be employed upon your body.

Interrogators from mediaeval times onwards have long known the value of their victims' imagination. I recently read a history of the Inquisition from which one passage has stuck in my mind: 'The accused would then be shown the various contraptions of torture… the majority broke down easily and the application of the machines was unnecessary.'

Being somewhat more civilised than the Inquisition, I prefer to think of this worrying anticipation as a form of foreplay, an exciting interlude before our quasi-sexual encounter commences. Many first-time clients, particularly the women and couples, wander nervously around the room. They study but rarely dare to touch the large and scary pieces of equipment and the displays of clamps, hoods, gas-masks, open-mouthed dental gags and intriguing medical instruments that line the walls. The men tend to sit quietly, awaiting their fate. Could it be that women are simply the more naturally curious gender, or possibly that they are the braver? The truth is that I've designed this waiting period to heighten your senses for what is to come. You and I are about to engage in a fascinating theatrical drama. I need you in the most receptive of moods to truly appreciate my grand entrance upon the stage.

In due course you hear the slow footfall of my high-heel boots on the stairs and the dungeon door opens. Experienced and well-trained devotees are by now prostrate on the polished wooden floor, not daring to meet their beloved Mistress's gaze. But for the newer admirers among you there will be a warm and welcoming smile. I wish to sit for a moment and put you at your ease with 'a little chat'. For me, this is one of the most important moments of our time together. I'll already know how long a session you've booked and the type of services you are seeking. This is now your opportunity – your *only* opportunity – to elaborate on your most secret desires. The more honest you are, the more you will benefit from the hours that lie ahead. Years of experience have given me the ability to see beyond what you say, to interpret your innermost thoughts and to decide on the best shape of the session to come. There is nothing you can say that might shock me; the panoply of the kinky extremes of human sexual activity has been laid before me many times before. It may well be that I gently remind you of the few activities in which I will *not* engage but I never mind you asking. You must lay bare your soul to find out what is, or isn't, possible.

We will also now discuss the use of your 'safeword' or phrase you can utter if you truly want our games to stop. Some of my more experienced followers, the ones who have earned the status of being an owned 'slave', delight in *not* employing a safeword; they have absolute trust in my ability to accurately judge their levels of distress and to temper my torments to suit their psychological and physical limits. For most of my clients, however, the knowledge that they can use their safeword in extremis is a reassuring backstop. There's little fun to be had, for example, from suffering muscle cramps in the middle of a lengthy bondage game or of holding back an overwhelming need to pee while suspended in straps from the ceiling. A safeword will bring you much-needed relief – in all senses of the word – in either of those unfortunate circumstances.

Now that our initial interview is over, I alone will decide what will happen to your body and your mind over the next hour… or two… or three. Your treatment may require a visit to my medical chambers, my suspension room, or my cells. In each of these rooms you will usually be kept in the strictest of bondage, restrained by ropes, or chains, or trapped within the confines of a leather strait jacket or one of my many rubber body-bags wrapped snugly around your body. The choice of material is yours, the severity and duration of the bondage will be mine. Depending on your desires, you may or may not be in pain; some clients crave the bite of my nipple clamps, the sting of my whip or the dull ache of excited confinement within a tight metal chastity belt. Others prefer a gentler experience, the floating feeling of being suspended from my body board as it is winched effortlessly into the air, the claustrophobic touch of a leather mask strapped tightly across the face, or the incessant throb of an electric butt-plug inserted into their rear.

Whatever your torment of choice, your role is now simplicity itself: you will obey instantly my every command and suffer or be pleasured precisely as I, and I alone, may wish. Our time for talking is over – indeed this is often a good moment for me to introduce a gag and pump it up sufficiently to ensure your silent acquiescence in our game. You are now at the mercy of my creative skills, my long experience in the dark arts of domination and my skilled and caring hands. Many players use the expression 'power exchange' to describe the experience and, although it is not a term I use often, it does sum up what has occurred between us. You have given me absolute power over your body and mind. I have accepted it. Let us explore together how corrupting that can be.

There are distinct differences between the way that men and women react when I share such details about what I do for a living. Men are often overcome with shyness, have no idea what to say to me and rapidly descend into a tongue-tied mumble of confusion. They may come up with the stock question for all workers in the 'adult' industry: 'What's a nice girl like you doing in a job like this?' By contrast, women are usually overcome with curiosity from the start. 'What do you actually *do?'* they ask. 'Do you tie people up? Spank their bottoms? Whip their backsides?' Or, as one of my relatives once famously asked: 'Do you *really* touch men's willies?' as though doing such a thing would never have occurred to her in a million years.

The answer of course is 'all of the above' – and much, much more – albeit with the ever-present health protection of an endless supply of medical-grade latex gloves. Within my chambers you can be prodded and probed, exposed and explored, bound and beaten. Far more important than any of the physical contact, however, is the psychological impact I have on the minds of my male and female clients. I pride myself on taking submissive men and women on private journeys to explore areas of their sexuality where fantasy rules... and pain and pleasure intermingle. I can give you an idea of what happens in my sessions with recent, real-life examples of the games that I play: firstly with one of my regular male clients, secondly with a girl who visits sporadically when she feels a need to be dominated by another woman, and lastly with a couple who regularly experience the delights of my chambers together.

CHAPTER 3

THOSE WHO PLAY TOGETHER... STAY TOGETHER

Picking a random man to best represent my customer base proved harder than I'd imagined. Looking back on recent sessions, I realised that sexual tastes, individual perversions and everyone's experience with BDSM activities vary so widely that it's hard to settle on any 'average' client. In the end I opted for Colin, obviously a pseudonym (as are all the names of clients in this book), but a real man who worked in the legal profession, as do quite a few of my clients. What is it about working as a lawyer that predisposes one to be submissive?

Colin is intelligent, educated, good company, well-travelled and comparatively wealthy. He is in his mid-fifties, married with grown-up children, and although I have, of course, never mixed with him in normal society, I do not doubt for a moment that he is a pillar of his local community. He also adores the feel, the scent and the texture of rubber against his naked skin. He has described his need to me on many occasions over the years: 'I start to think about rubber, how it feels and smells and then begin to imagine what we did on the last occasion I saw you. I play each session back in my mind, sometimes masturbating to the memory of being covered in a rubber bag or a sheet and playing in my mind with the sensations I felt at that time. I don't feel ashamed of wanting this but it is not something that I could ever share with anyone at all – and certainly not with my wife. I don't think she'd understand but, even if she did, it's not something I could share with her. Eventually, even though I have tried not to see you so often, I can't resist picking up the phone and calling your number. Then the anticipation builds to fever pitch as the day of my appointment gets closer.'

Colin appears on my bookings list with great regularity, once a month or so, when his desire for latex encasement and a certain level of discipline begins to overwhelm his senses. In the immediate aftermath of a lengthy rubber session with me he is content to resume normal life and normal 'vanilla' sex with his partner... for a while. Then, rather like a reformed smoker requiring a nicotine fix, he feels the need to turn up once again at my door. Like many of my clients, Colin has no real idea as to *why* he enjoys his particular fetish. Examining his childhood reveals no credible clues to explain his desires, and he has no real interest in finding out more. He has the money, the freedom and the inclination to explore his deepest desires with me and feels comfortable about doing just that. His sessions tend to follow a set pattern, although I strive to introduce a new element into the scene on every visit. The insertion of a 'wild card' moment into the mix keeps the games fresh and, more importantly, safeguards me against the danger of boredom. I love my job and I love the way I can enhance each person's desires by adding in activities or fantasies pulled from my own imagination. Without that element of creativity, my role would be mechanical and repetitive; it is my sexual imagination that makes it exciting, rewarding and fun.

For a typical session, Colin will strip naked and dress in some of the vast selection of rubber clothes that hang in my dungeon's wardrobes. Elbow-high rubber gloves, full-length rubber stockings, a tight-fitting but open-face rubber hood, a rubber jerkin, and possibly rubber chaps covering his lower limbs but leaving both his backside and genitalia exposed and available. Depending on my own mood I may leave him to dress himself, or fuss around him, dictating exactly what I want him to wear, whether he likes it or not. It's fascinating to see his manner change as each rubber layer is applied. Before my eyes, Colin changes from a confident and slightly brash solicitor to a humble and obedient slave, desperate to obey my every instruction. There's no need for shouting or harsh words with him, his desperation to please me binds him to my will.

By now, Colin's hands have been secured out of the way; he's encased in latex and enjoying every moment of the scene. But I am not called The Bondage Mistress for nothing. His rubber experience has barely just begun. I've already chosen a second hood to go over his head. My selection ranges from terrifying, heavy rubber bags with the smallest of air-holes, through to numerous gas masks and hoods. My current favourite is an elaborate German design in which air may only be drawn in through multiple tubes attached to a 'smell-bag' container strapped to Colin's chest. The smell-bag does just what it says on the tin – scented items of any description can be placed in the bag to swamp the wearer with the chosen aroma. The contents are limited only by my imagination, although it may not surprise you to know that my worn, rubber thongs are a particular delight for many of my slaves. Depending on the design of hood which I've chosen I might then add a rubber pump-up gag with a breathing tube, a tightly restricting collar and even a rubber blindfold.

In Colin's case, even such an extreme outfit is rarely enough. He needs strapping down to my medical bench and tucking up tight with one or more heavy rubber blankets around his head and body. Only when every inch of his body is pressed down under multiple layers of latex will I consider offering some form of sexual relief. I'll sometimes attach him to my 'milking' machine, a converted agricultural unit once employed on milking Friesians but now capable of masturbating and sucking up to four slaves at once. It rarely takes Colin long to achieve the desired result if I decide that his good behaviour has earned him an orgasm.

By contrast with my difficulties in choosing an average man, an easy choice presents itself when it comes to couples. I love playing with couples; they are always such good fun. Sometimes, if they are living and playing together as a couple in real life, they bring their own equipment which will always excite me. As an equipment and sexual gadget junkie, I adore anything new I can get my hands on: 'Oh please let me have a go.' On occasions, both partners are submissive and then I can have the titillation of linking them together in bondage.

THOSE WHO PLAY TOGETHER... STAY TOGETHER

Jonathon and Elaine are an unlikely pairing who really know how to party. Both married, but not to each other, they met on a BDSM internet website and come together only for sex and domination games. Both cheating on their straight-sex partners, they are the perfect example of the way in which the internet and a desire for 'unusual' sex can connect people who would otherwise never have met. Today's more public face of BDSM is perhaps the reason why more and more couples now visit my chambers together. I've always had a preponderance of male clients, although lone women are far from unknown. Now there's a noticeable trend towards the idea that 'couples who play together stay together'.

Elaine is a charming, flirtatious, highly submissive young lady; Jonathon, 20 years older, is equally charming and switches between the roles of dominant and submissive with consummate ease. I sometimes session with Jonathon on his own but Elaine only visits West London Towers in Jonathan's company. I described her above as submissive but that's not quite correct; she is a confirmed masochist who sometimes refuses to submit at all. She can be defiant and cheeky in order to goad Jonathon and me into increasing the severity of whichever punishment she is suffering at the time.

On one visit, Jonathon tied Elaine, naked, to the medical bench and spread her legs apart in the gynaecological stirrups. Her blindfold prevented her from seeing who might be touching her or what might happen to her next. As arranged with Jonathon, I left him to play with her for a while but then slipped silently into the room to run my rubber-gloved hands across her helpless body. I could see she was desperately trying to work out what was happening as two hands started caressing her nipples and a further two hands delved between her legs. The hands pinching her nipples were Jonathon's; the hands stroking her clitoris were mine. Now I should perhaps say here that I am completely heterosexual in my private life. I can appreciate when a woman is attractive, but I am not attracted myself. In my own wildest fantasies I am always surrounded by men – preferably about a dozen of them all playing with me at any one time – but I have no problems in dominating women if it enhances the fun of couples who are paying for my time.

On this occasion though, Elaine was not there to be lovingly caressed; she was seeking pain and discomfort and that's something I'm always happy to provide. She had never experienced needle-play – something of a speciality of mine – and I wanted to introduce her to those new sensations. Before inserting the finest of needles, scrupulously sterile and obtained from a leading medical equipment supplier, I cleaned her breasts with alcohol swabs. Elaine's blindfold had by then already been removed so that she might fully anticipate what was about to happen; as always, it is the prospect of pain, more than the pain itself, which starts the adrenaline pumping. With fingers clad in surgeons' latex gloves I carefully inserted a needle on either side of each nipple. She winced and whimpered as each point broke the skin but was clearly enjoying both the pain and the sight of her nipples now interlaced with the gleam of metal pins. My final task was to push the needle tips into two small corks; I would hate any of my clients, or me, to jab themselves unnecessarily.

Seeking to bring the couple's session to a suitably climatic end, I donned one of my biggest strap-on cocks and positioned myself between Elaine's thighs. Jonathon had readied his video camera to record the abuse I was about to inflict on his partner. I have an enormous variety of rubber, plastic, and even metal dildos available to use on either men or women. Some are rock hard plastic, some are made of softer rubber and quite a few of them vibrate. They all fit interchangeably into a custom-made leather and elasticised strap harness which sits securely around my waist and thighs to give me a faux erection of which any man would be proud. This ever-ready penis collection comes in a variety of colours, although that never seems to be of much importance to male clients – perhaps because they are often blindfolded or because I am usually standing behind them when I put them to use. Women, however, seem to care far more about the visual impact of a scene and so it was for Elaine's benefit that I was that evening wearing a particularly fetching pink cock which I knew would stretch her to her limits.

I took my time ensuring that the dildo sat securely in my harness and then took even longer ostentatiously lubricating the tip and the shaft of the erect member in order to increase the theatricality of the occasion. So much of what I do in my sessions is, in reality, pure theatre; a carefully choreographed performance designed to heighten my clients' sexual desire and therefore their subsequent pleasure. It's never enough so simply spank, or crop or cane a man's behind for example; far better to render him helpless, warm his rear with some stylishly delivered slaps from my hand and then allow him to watch as I take my time in selecting the next implement from a hook on the wall. I'll be chatting to him or just to myself throughout the process: 'Hmm… now let me see, this crop might be good… or perhaps this one… it's a little whippier and more painful… which is just what you need.' Performing like an actress on stage is, of course, also the reason why I have wardrobes full of exotic and erotic rubber and leather uniforms, along with racks of thigh-high boots and stiletto-heeled shoes. All are needed for the constant costume changes required to keep the Miranda Show up and running: numerous performances a week, and matinee appearances on demand.

However, returning to my couple's story, I could hear Jonathan's breathing grow heavier and see that his excitement levels were visibly burgeoning as I readied Elaine for penetration. He was having trouble holding his camera steady as I gently eased my faux-cock between her outer vulva lips and pushed in to the hilt. After an hour of steadily increasing pain and discomfort, Elaine was more than ready to receive me. Like all true masochists, her excitement increases with each step up her personal pain ladder as a session progresses. Her pain is no less unpleasant than it would be to you or to me, but, for her, the sensation of pain translates into sexual pleasure. To increase her fun further I pressed a vibrator against the hood of her clitoris and told Jonathon to lightly touch the needles piercing each of her areola. It was a combination of pain and pleasure which I knew Elaine would be unable to resist: in due course, she proved me right.

Her climax – which, although I say it myself, was a rather spectacular example of my work – left one person in the room still frustrated and desperate for relief. Poor Jonathan was begging for one of us girls to lend him a hand. Elaine, who clearly was used to doing his bidding, duly reached out and started to stroke him. My urgent command stopped her in her tracks: 'No... Elaine, don't touch. He hasn't earned any pleasure... and he is not getting a climax tonight.' A look of desperation crossed Jonathan's face but he knows better than to argue with his Mistress once a decision has been made. I'm amazed that women don't always appreciate the power of sometimes leaving a man frustrated and desperate to ejaculate. They may get a little sulky and stomp around for a bit but that mood passes, leaving them compliant and attentive enough to make any woman happy.

Having dealt with 'typical' male and couples clients, that leaves one other category unaccounted for – the single women who occasionally fall into my hands (ignoring for a moment the many men who come to me seeking to be made-up and dressed as a woman). Women do add a spice of variety to life but I can't deny that they can be hard work. Perhaps it's because I am a heterosexual woman that I find pleasuring a man to be a relatively simple affair. A few rapid strokes, a little verbal erotica to get his heart racing and voila: a climax is almost guaranteed. Much of the time one doesn't even need a full erection; what could possibly be easier? Women, on the other hand, exhibit a bewildering multitude of variations when it comes to exciting their ladyparts. In my professional life I've tried every possible method of bringing a woman to orgasm. I've employed my latex-gloved fingers, a mixture of pain and pleasure, erotic stories, penetration at every possible depth and speed, my variable-speed fucking machine, the tongues of my willing male slaves, and vibrators of every shape and size. Some women do come easily, over and over again, while others struggle to reach that moment at all, despite hours of patient work by their partners. No one method guarantees success and it is only when a woman tries giving another woman an orgasm that she appreciates the problems men face throughout their lives.

However, one female client fortunately proved to have no difficulty whatsoever in finding sexual satisfaction at my hands. Lorraine is a professional lap-dancer and television adult-channel performer with a body to die for. A genuine submissive and masochist, she likes me to push her limits a little further with each visit. I adore variety above all else in my sexual games and Lorraine gives me ample chance to employ a little-used technique to give her the pain she desires. She is a particular fan of bastinado, the ancient torture of caning the soles of the feet. Her tolerance for the pain this produces is astonishingly high, as one of my male slaves learned to his cost. He should never have agreed to take part in a filmed foot-caning contest between himself and Lorraine.

To make things easier for me, I tied the male submissive to my whipping bench and strapped Lorraine to my bondage throne, a convenient arms-length away. Each had their bare feet raised and perfectly presented for the blows to come. The winner was to be the one who lasted longest before having to use his or her safeword (as described earlier) to bring the contest to a close. As always, I began the session gently and then steadily increased the torment they were required to endure. I have found over the years that this gradual progression through any form of play or punishment is essential to get the best from my slaves. Many novice Mistresses – and, I am sad to say, some experienced ones as well – seemingly fail to understand the importance of that rule. Given that the purpose of the game is to help the slave explore to the full his or her own sexual desire, there seems little point in steaming in so hard that limits of endurance are reached within moments. A little patience pays considerable dividends.

To that end, I began my bastinado Olympics by employing a light flogger with multiple strands of soft suede which sting but cause no serious pain. Both of my contestants knew me well enough to have realised that this was but the first stage of this unusual type of podiatry. Indeed, as is my wont, I had laid out a small selection of different instruments on the bench where both contestants could see them. Anticipation is all. We progressed to a more punishing riding crop, moved up a gear through one or two of the lighter, whippier canes and then onto the heaviest cane which I was confident would sort out the men from the boys. So it proved to be. The first few swipes across the sole of his foot soon dragged the safeword from my male subbie's lips. Lorraine had a little smile of triumph on her face as she heard her male companion cry out 'for his mummy' – the particularly humiliating phrase that I make him use as a safeword when he truly needs me to stop.

It had proved to be no-contest, with my female champion easily dispatching her opponent inside a few rounds. The loser was sent from the room and I decided that Lorraine's prize was to be a session on the medical bench with multiple needles through various tender parts of her body. This was new to Lorraine and although she tolerated a few needles through her nipples, I soon discovered her limits as the first metal tip touched the skin of her labia majora. With real tears of fear running down her cheeks, Lorraine begged me to stop but I knew she could take more if she tried. I had already laid out the exact number of needles ready to be inserted and in such cases I work on the same principle as those governing the Samurai warriors of ancient Japan. Legend has it that a Samurai sword, once unsheathed, cannot be put away without being used: and so it is with me. Once the needles are ready and waiting they have to find a home. In such situations I have found that a calm but utterly determined tone of voice can encourage any slave further along the path of complete submission than they may have expected.

'You are going to take more needles, young lady,' I insisted. 'I know you don't want to… and I know they hurt, but you do want to please me, don't you? That's why these needles are going in now… then we can get this nasty stage over and done with and move on. That's what we all want, isn't it?'

My script may sound ineffective when viewed in cold print, but whispered close to a slave's ear, with the correct tone of voice and the authority that I've spent decades perfecting, it works every time. I backed up my words with actions by popping my half-a-dozen remaining needles right through her outer labia lips to accompanying squeals of pain from my now-quiescent client. Even now, Lorraine's fun was not over. I pointed out that the unsheathed needle points were now resting gently on her inner vaginal lips and that any movement from her would likely result in a fascinating but unusual self-piercing experience. 'I suggest you lay *very* still,' I instructed as I left the room. 'Don't move and I'll be back in a while to set you free.' Still nervous, still shaking a little and still crying, Lorraine had little choice. She meekly accepted her fate.

Examining the enjoyment I received from ill-treating my slavegirl, I realised that I do get a thrill from imposing my will over her, from making her obey my commands, with appropriate discipline and encouragement if required. There is, however, a huge difference between the reward I get from dominating a woman and the sexual charge I can get from dealing with a man. As a heterosexual, I still get my own sexual kick out of sessions with any male, even after two decades of practicing just about every imaginable form of domination game. I've never been one for self-reflection or for analysing why I am the way I am, so I don't know why it is that I relish submission from others in both my professional and personal lives. The debate between 'nature and nurture' seems to me to be a mystery with so many variables that no answer will ever be found.

Even so, I do recognise that my life has taken an unusual course and that this might well be related to my somewhat unusual childhood. It was a happy childhood, running smoothly for years... until the day I discovered that all of my happiness was built on a lie.

CHAPTER 4

'YOUR MUMMY ISN'T REALLY YOUR MUMMY'

As is the case for many of us, my life thus far has been an ever-changing mix of joy, happiness, sadness and occasional despair. Yet, looking back over the decades, one day in the spring of 1983 stands out as one of the worst moments of my entire life. I've never forgotten the cold, sinking feeling in the pit of my nine-year-old tummy as my best friend at school uttered words that broke my heart.

'Everyone knows – except you of course – your mummy isn't *really* your mummy.'

Seeing the words in print cannot convey the sheer, ice-cold fear that gripped me as I struggled to absorb and understand the words my friend was speaking. What on earth could she mean? What a silly thing to say, what a stupid lie to tell. Or was it a lie? Of course I loved my mummy dearly: as is the case for all young children, she was the heart of my schoolgirl world. How was it possible that the certainty of such a relationship could now be threatened? I was fighting back the tears as I ran home in a daze to what I believed was the emotional safety of my parents' home.

Bursting in through our never-locked back door I found my mummy in our tiny kitchen, fresh from work at another local school and still dressed in her dinner-lady uniform of grey skirt, pure white blouse and blue tabard – a necessity to protect herself from the soup splashes and chaos of serving lunches to scores of secondary-school children. Although my friend had upset me, I was sure that Mummy would soon take the scary feeling of uncertainty away... wouldn't she?

How wrong can one be?

I had been a blissfully happy little girl until that afternoon when my loving childhood world fell apart. It was the day I found out that all the adults I knew, and all the grown-ups I loved and I trusted, had been lying to me throughout my young life. It had started like any other, with my normal lessons at school, and with me trying my hardest to please my teachers. One teacher always joked that if she set me one page of writing to do, she would always get back five. I remember people telling me I was 'a bright little thing', and so lessons were easy and fun. It was an ethnically-diverse school set between two huge West London council house estates, and I was always the tallest and skinniest girl in my class. I usually came near the top of the form in any tests, which was enough to make me a favourite target for the school bully, a little boy, no older than me, who would call me names and who sometimes waited after school to tease me, push me across the path and try to make my cry. It was simply schoolyard stuff and never a serious problem but the man I knew as my dad was angry when he found me sniffling into my hankie one day after my classmate bully had teased me outside the school gates.

Strong, wiry, handsome, always loving, and totally dependable, my grandfather – who I had grown up knowing as my dad – was one of the two rocks on which my young life was built. He had a great sense of humour and was always laughing and joking. His naturally wavy hair smelt of Bryclreem and was a source of considerable pride. 'You know all you girls want hair like mine,' he would tell me, an unlikely supposition given that my own hair was so long I could sit on it. After years of service in the Royal Navy, my grandfather had been made redundant and was at home a great deal as he struggled to find another job. Although I did not understand his unemployment at the time, his house-husband role meant that he and I grew even closer. I felt I was lucky to have a daddy always at home, while other friends had to wait until almost bedtime before their fathers came home to play.

For my grandfather, the bullying incident was easy to deal with: 'You just have to stand up for yourself, darling. Push the boy back, you're bigger than him anyway. Punch him if you have to. I'll teach you how you can fight.' To my mum's – or rather grandmother's – horror, she walked into the house after work to a scene in which Granddad was play-fighting with me in the living-room, teaching me a flat-handed chop to the side of the neck that he guaranteed would win any fight. 'Don't teach her things like that,' she pleaded. 'She'll go and kill the boy, instead of stopping him bullying.' In the event, the lesson worked a treat. The very next day I turned the tables on my previously-feared tormentor. Although never utilising the much-hyped 'Navy Death Blow', I did walk up to the boy after school, full of the confidence my grandfather had given me. I pushed him as hard as I could; he fell on his back, picked himself up… and ran away crying. Looking back now, I feel (just a little) ashamed of the way that my new-found power over him developed from that point. I was now the one who waited for him after school and teased and tormented him to the point of tears. On one memorable afternoon, I made him kneel down on the path and kiss my school shoes – the first of the innumerable times that men have since literally worshipped at my feet.

Being bullied was to play no part, however, in the awful day when I first learned about what I have always thought of as the BIG LIE. After school that afternoon I had walked home, as I often did, with my best friend, Susie. She was a plump, friendly, but always-naughty little girl of my own age, who lived near our small, semi-detached house on a London suburban council estate. I think at the time she qualified as my 'best, best' friend. It was cold, cloudy April weather and, as usual, my house was chilly and damp.

One of my abiding memories as a child is of always being cold in that house. It was an old council property; the type now euphemistically termed 'social housing'. It was a form of social housing in my day too; so cold in winter that huddling together for warmth in a highly 'social' way was the only means of keeping warm. The house is now long gone, and good riddance too, with its lack of any cavity walls, no insulation, no double-glazing and no trace of anything that

could remotely be described as central heating. I remember
visiting friends in the winter and desperately trying to eke out
my stay for as long as possible in order to avoid returning to
my own freezing bedroom. There were times when the house
seemed colder inside than out and I hesitated to get into bed
because of the chilled, clammy feeling of the sheets. I have
long suffered from, thankfully mild, asthma, probably not
unrelated to the fact that mould grew unchecked on the damp
bathroom walls of my home. My friends now are well aware
of my constant need to be warm. That lust for heat comes
from growing up in a room where, rather than wipe
condensation from the windows, one sometimes had to scrape
ice from the *inside* of the glass before being able to see what
the weather might be doing outside.

Because her house was always warmer, Susie and I settled
down in her small bedroom to play. Whatever our games were
on any particular day, we two seemed always to be talking,
silly conversations about childhood things, and make-believe
games of being grown-up and what we might do, who we
might marry, and where we might live. But this afternoon was
different. Susie had a secret to share.

The night before, Susie's mummy had been chatting to an
elderly neighbour who lived in our street. I still remember the
woman well, she was the local busybody, shrew-faced, always
a bit miserable and with rarely a kind word to say about
anything to anyone. Susie had overheard their entire
conversation, and was desperate to tell me her news: 'Your
mummy's not really your mummy,' she said. 'And your daddy
isn't really your daddy, your real daddy lives over the road
with your real nan and granddad, and your big sister isn't

really your sister, and it's all what my mummy calls "a God-Almighty mess". And you are... a *bastard* little girl.'

Susie was just excited by her news, blurting out her new secret with words that were never meant to be as harsh and unkind as they sound on this page. And neither she nor I had any real understanding of what a 'bastard' was. But we knew it was a naughty, nasty name that grown-ups called each other. As each new revelation tumbled from her lips, I found myself struggling to understand, overwhelmed with a growing sense of horror and disbelief, and fighting a losing battle as I tried hard not to cry. Finally, with tears now streaming down my face, I ran, as fast as fast could be, down Susie's stairs and straight out of her front door. Hurrying across the road and into my own house, I rushed past the two people I had always known as mother and father in the kitchen and took the stairs two-at-a-time. As I threw myself, sobbing, face down on the bed in the sanctuary of my own little boxroom bedroom, my horrified mum was hot on my heels.

'Miranda... darling... what on earth is wrong? Why are you crying? Are you hurt? What's the matter?'

It took many minutes of her cuddling, holding and reassuring me for me to find the strength to stop crying and give her some sort of answer. I knew that my mummy would make it all better: Susie must have been making-up stories, must have been repeating nasty lies about me, she must have been mistaken. But, when I told my mum what my little friend had said, there was a horrified, and horrifying, silence.

'I thought you knew darling, we did tell you before, when you were little. Don't you remember?'

Looking back now, more than 30 years later, into the

depths of my memory, I still am not sure if I do remember any of their babyhood explanations or not. Apparently, I had been told as an infant, perhaps just two years old, that my 'real' mother was leaving home and that I was to be looked after by my maternal grandparents. I was told that I had been 'adopted' by my nan and granddad, and that they would care for me now that my real mummy had moved away. My family then assumed that, with duty done, there was no point in repeating the explanation when I grew a little older. 'Least said, soonest mended,' seems to have been their watchword without ever considering that such traumatic news would have been blanked out of my little-girl mind as though no words had ever been spoken in the first place.

It may be that I had retained some sub-conscious worry that all in my family life was not quite what it seemed. I remember being puzzled that other children knew more about the time and the exact circumstances of their own birth. That uncertainty was perhaps the reason why I would occasionally ask my mum gentle questions about it: 'Oh, how much did I weigh when I was born, Mum?'

'Well… I just don't remember exactly now Miranda. That's a silly question… I'm not sure… it was a long time ago because you're a grown girl now.'

How odd it was that my mum couldn't remember my birth weight, I used to think. Naturally, I can recognise now that whatever she did or did not remember, such issues were always brushed aside and my attention quickly deflected on to other things. Then again, perhaps I never had the courage to ask the direct questions that might have proved both more illuminating and more painful: 'Susie's mum tells her all about when she was born. If you had me then why don't you remember?' Might it have been that even at that young age I was colluding in my own childish way with my family's conspiracy of silence? Might I have been unwittingly conspiring to keep myself in the dark?

Whatever the truth of my own complicity, the fact is that from the moment I was originally told the story of my adoption, 'the scandal' was never spoken of again. And, even if I had once heard what the adults thought they were telling me, the memory had been utterly lost in those seemingly-endless years of early childhood – till the day when Susie revealed her big secret. It was thus a devastating moment when I realised that her fantastical story was true. My mummy was not denying it and so many things were falling into place: an instant explanation as to why my mother and father were older than all my friends' parents, why Dad had so much grey in his handsome, dark hair, why Mum dyed her hair blonde to cover up her roots. I remember, vividly, lying face down on my bed and crying till I thought my heart would burst because I realised that I was the only one who did not know the truth. Yet, how could Mummy and Daddy not be Mummy and Daddy any longer? Why had everyone lied to me? Why did everyone else know all about me when I did not even know myself? Even my best friend, her whole family, and, as it later transpired, most of the people in my road, knew intimate secrets of which I had no knowledge. I was far from being old enough to vocalise such thoughts at the time but I did feel an overwhelming sense of betrayal and deceit.

Many years later, my grandmother – whom I still called 'my

mum' till the very day she died – told me how terrifying that afternoon had been for her and my grandfather. 'I suppose you might want to go and live with Eileen [my birth-mother] now?' she had said.

'No of course not,' I had tearfully replied. 'Why would I ever want to do that?'

But later, as I lay sobbing on my bed, they were crying in each other's arms in their own bedroom next door. Having failed to find any way of comforting their precious little 'daughter', they shared a fear that must be common to many adoptive parents. Now I knew who my 'real' mother was, and now I knew that she still lived less than an hour's drive from my house with a new young family, might I demand that we all be reunited? After years of caring and raising me as their own, this loving couple were scared that the girl they thought of only as their own little daughter might suddenly vanish from their lives. It was to be a long time before they lost that particular fear.

Finding out such a momentous truth as I had that day, at an age when one can start to understand the ramifications, is an astonishing experience. Every family relationship you think you have straight in your head is thrown out of the window. My mummy was suddenly my grandma, and my daddy was my granddad. My sister was my mother, her husband was my step-father, my cousins were my brother and sister, my other big sister was suddenly my aunt with her children promoting themselves instantly from nephew and niece to yet more cousins. I instantly had a new little brother and a new little sister. And where was my real daddy in all this… and my real nan and grandpa, on the other side of my family?

Amidst such confusion it is perhaps not surprising that in my soon-to-come teenage years, my sweet little Miranda-wagon would soon be running off of the rails.

CHAPTER 5

LEFT BEHIND

I still thought of my grandparents as my mum and dad, as indeed they legally were because they adopted me at the age of two or three shortly before Eileen, my birth-mother left home. I loved my nan and granddad dearly and would never suggest for a moment that they failed to give me the most loving childhood they could. Equally truthfully, however, I can't pretend that I had same upbringing as my siblings and most of my peers at school. When one's parents are in reality one's grandparents there are significant, yet subtle differences that conspire towards presenting a unique experience of childhood. A combination of their greater age, their old-fashioned attitudes and their relative poverty left me feeling that for me, life was different from that of others my age. It wasn't that I was jealous or envious of other children; just that I was always aware of the differences

In retrospect, I can also see that my grandparents' own knowledge of the truth of our relationship might sometimes have influenced their attitude to me. I have never doubted their total love and devotion, but having suddenly to raise a young child must at times have brought them heartache as well as love. They never showed any resentment towards my unexpected invasion of their late middle-age but surely there must have been occasions when it must have have felt, albeit for fleeting moments, I was a fledgling cuckoo in their nest?

I have no more than the vaguest of memories of the day that my 'big sister' left home and left me in the care of the couple who were to become the only mum and dad I've ever known. My deeper understanding of what happened has come over the years from various members of the family. I've been told that during the first couple of years of my life my birth-mother, the woman I've always known by her first name, Eileen, did look after and care for me at my grandparents' house. Apparently, at that age, I knew her as 'my mummy' – a crucial fact, of course, that was rapidly forgotten as I grew from an infant into a child. (These days, when speaking of my birth-mother I invariably refer to her simply *as* my birth-mother, rather than 'Mum' or 'Eileen'.)

I later learned from my birth-mother that she was just 15 when she fell pregnant, although she didn't recognise her condition until several months later, after her sixteenth birthday. Even when she was five months' pregnant she apparently sported a 22-inch waist and it was only after that, as her tummy grew, that her pregnancy was revealed. It was far too late by then for abortion to be an option. Eileen has told me that I was probably conceived the very first time she made love with her then boyfriend, a local lad who was her first serious boyfriend and her 'first love'. Although they had been seeing each other for a while, her parents had never been keen on the relationship because they thought he was both undesirable and unreliable. He treated her well when they were together but would often disappear from her life with little explanation, returning to pick up the friendship again when it suited him. After I was born, she did have contact with him but he would still leave for weeks at a time. Finally her parents had discouraged him from having anything to do with the baby and encouraged Eileen to stop seeing him because he was so unreliable and they insisted that she needed more stability in her life.

For the first couple of years of my life Eileen lived in the bedroom next door to my tiny, nursery room in her parents' West London home. She looked after me with the help of her own mother and our mother-child relationship was little different from that of any other. In the depths of my memory I have the tiniest snippets, like snapshot photographs in my head, of her being there; her smile perhaps and little moments like walking into her room and watching her doing her hair. But, because her parents were eager to share baby-sitting duties, my birth-mother could live a relatively normal teenage social life. In time she met and fell in love with another boy. Eventually that boy asked her to leave home and marry him.

The big unanswered question was: 'What to do about me?' My natural mother's answer was… to leave me behind.

When I've thought about it through the years, I've tried to hide away the trauma of that decision. It's been hard sometimes to know that my birth-mother was able to abandon her first-born child. How could she not have taken me with her to live with her new husband? Why did she not send for me a few years later when she had another couple of children – my half-brother and sister – and when I might still have made the transition back to be part of her family? The truth is that, despite the effect it had on my life, it is hard now for me to criticise decisions made so long ago and in such pressurised circumstances.

Eileen has told me many times that she regrets her decision to leave me behind. But she was only a teenager and had a forceful mother and father telling her what was for the best; how could she have done differently? My nan and granddad were enjoying their new role as surrogate parents, I was settled and apparently happy in their home and they could offer a loving and stable upbringing for their beloved granddaughter. My birth-mother may well have been weak but I do believe she thought she was acting for the best.

I have long accepted that everybody at the time did what they thought was right and were acting with the best of intentions. And yet lingering doubts do remain. When Eileen tells me now that she wishes I had lived with her, it is hard not to think, 'Well, why didn't you say so at the time? Why didn't you fight for me? When you had a new family, why didn't you take me in then?'

There is a family story of the day that Eileen left me with her parents. Apparently she swore that if I cried when she left she would be unable to walk out of the door and would have to take me with her. That upset was side-stepped by my grandmother who took me off into the back garden so that I would not have to see my mum walk out of the door... and she would not see any tears. Even before she left, my birth-mother had signed adoption papers to make the arrangement legal. I've never seen a copy of my original birth certificate which my grandmother apparently destroyed. Many years later when I wanted a passport I applied for a birth-certificate copy. It is a surprisingly short and little-detailed document, failing to record my mother or father's names and merely stating the date of my birth and that I am, thankfully, 'a female'.

At some time soon after Eileen had left, I simply forgot who she was. It's hard to understand how any child can forget their own mum, you might think. But I, of course, did have a mum and a dad, in the shape of my grandparents. They became my whole childish world and my reality: so much so that when Eileen got married shortly afterwards I was recruited as a bridesmaid. Far from recalling that event as my mother's marriage, I can remember only that I was as pretty as a picture in a new pink dress. The significance of the actual event had, by then, totally passed me by.

That was all long before I rediscovered the truth about why my 'mum and dad' were so much older than me. One girl at my school did have an astonishingly young mother. She seemed like a baby compared with my own mum: so young, highly attractive, lively and full of energy. I remember her as going out to parties all the time, being very trendy and 'hip', a huge contrast with my own mother's life. As far as I could see only one other person in my class had parents anywhere near as old as my mum and dad. Her name was Amanda and, partly because we both had elderly mums, and partly because my mother earned a few extra shillings by child-minding Amanda

43

after school, we became close friends. Amanda had two far older siblings and she confided in me she'd been told she was 'a late addition to the family by mistake'. I believed that I must have been a similar 'late addition by mistake' despite ever really understanding what that meant. What I did know was that other children, who will seize on any slight differences to tease and annoy, were only too happy to take the mickey out of me for having an 'old mum'. I was glad that Amanda was around to share that particular burden.

The other reason for valuing Amanda's friendship was that I was painfully shy at that age and didn't always mix comfortably with other kids. It was not that I was unpopular, just that I rarely joined in with the crowd or sought to be a leading light in the group. I would talk to the others but if they were doing their group thing, what you might call 'girly games', then I did not want to know. If a sports game was in the offing, however, then I was always the first to be picked. I was ridiculously flexible, so was very good at gymnastics, and my height gave me an unbeatable advantage for netball. In our mixed school the boys were always playing football and asking me to join in their games. The speed at which I could run and the length I could jump kept me at the forefront of all the athletics as well. Without a family car and with ageing parents I rarely went on the sort of school-holiday outings that many of my friends seemed to enjoy. Instead you would find me most likely in our little back garden, messing around with the netball or trying to do some gymnastics, seeing for how long I could sustain a handstand or attempting the splits. Exercises and backflips on the lawn would keep me amused for hours on end.

I loved all sports and might in different circumstances have considered a sporting career, I still train several times a week with the help of a skilled, personal trainer and have always tried to keep myself as fit as possible. But any possibility of becoming a professional sportswoman foundered at school on the rocks of my parents' financial problems. Watching sport on television, I noticed that some people actually seemed to make their living from this one activity I loved, the one activity at which I truly excelled. Seeing gymnastics in particular I would ask my grandmother, 'How do these girls end up in competitions and stuff?' and she would reply 'Oh they've got personal trainers and do nothing but practice all day.'

'Wow... can I get a trainer and do that?'

'Oh, don't be silly Miranda, we haven't got the money for anything like that.'

I had endless enthusiasm to do a variety of things with my life but my grandmother had neither the money, nor the know-how, to encourage or pick-up on my interests.

None of the above means that my grandparents did not love me to pieces and I enjoyed a surfeit of emotional warmth and affection from them. Some of that may have come my way because my nan had herself been raised in an orphanage with no mother-love whatsoever after her own mother died and her father had remarried. She always told me that being in the orphanage was better than the abusive life she had led at home with her father and the original evil stepmother. My granddad had been in the Navy and had then worked at the local Hoover factory before being made redundant when I was very young. He was never able to work again because he suffered from chronic pulmonary obstructive disorder (COPD) which meant that his ability to breathe worsened progressively year after year. At heart he was a fun-loving person but as time passed he was completely struck down by the limitations of his illness. His lung capacity was terrible, really bad, so that even walking up a flight of stairs would cause him to puff and pant. In his later years all his efforts were expended in just trying to breathe, which cost him his sparkle and brought on depression. 'What bloody use am I to anyone? I can't do anything,' he would sometimes say. 'My bloody legs are no use to me at all, I can't go anywhere.'

I was asthmatic from an early age but never suffered remotely as much as my grandfather did. Whereas I might trigger an asthma attack by sudden exertions such as running for a bus, his breathing troubles were continuous and would leave him struggling for air in the day and coughing through the nights. His one regular pleasure was a trip to his local pub where he would play dominos and down a pint or two prior to coming home and falling asleep on the sofa. He used that pub for nearly 50 years and yet never had any sort of drink problem – he just enjoyed the company and the routine of that part of his life. Even so, some of my funniest childhood memories are of teasing him when he was a little too much the worse for wear before those afternoon naps. I would put all his hair in elastic hairbands as he slept and try to draw on him before my nan realised what I was doing. She took my joking in her normal good-natured way until the day I drew a picture of Granddad and wrote a note across it: 'Too Drunk To Remember.'

'That's not funny Miranda, it's just rude' scolded my nan. I still have the picture – complete with the replacement caption words with which I calmed her anger: 'God Save the Queen' was my slightly surreal attempt to get back into her good books. My grandfather loved children and when family came to stay he would welcome my cousins with open arms. He called us all 'bairns', a hangover from his upbringing in the north of England.

Much of the advice my granddad gave me throughout my childhood did stick and has been of use to me in my business life – even though I cannot always follow his golden rules on never getting into debt. 'Never borrow money Miranda; never lend money; do not get seduced into asking for credit; don't spend what you do not have.' It was a reflection of the fact that he was probably the most honest man I have ever known. In his younger days he passed examinations to be a police officer but the starting pay was then so low that, with a young family to look after, he could not afford to take the job. His grasp of mathematics was excellent and family legend has it that he was offered a grammar school place as a child but his parents had to turn it down because they couldn't afford the school uniform.

Much though I loved him, I cannot deny that among all of his good traits of forbearance and honesty, he did have a couple of faults. He could not let any argument end, other than on his terms. When we argued – as we did more frequently over the years – he would listen until I had finished every possible argument... and then jump in one last time with a little jibe in order that he had could be sure he had had the last word. He was also an obsessive hoarder, possibly from

47

being short of material of all kinds in the post-war period. My favourite item among the treasure trove of junk which sat untouched for years in his garden shed was a wooden dining room chair with only three legs.

'Why on earth are you keeping that chair?' my nan would demand.

'There's nothing wrong with it,' he would retort. 'All you need do is stick a piece of wood on to replace that leg and it'll be as good as new.'

'But you're never going to do that, are you?'

'Maybe not… but I just might.'

He and my grandmother thought the world of each other and there was a joy about growing up in a household where so much love was in the air. They were never openly affectionate towards each other – the idea of kissing in public would have shocked them to the core – but after a drink or two he would sneak a sly cuddle, only to be told: 'Johnny stop it right now, the children are watching.' Children were very important to my grandmother. In addition to loving me she would care for other children after school, earning a tiny extra bit of money to supplement the pittance she earned working part-time as a school dinner-lady. That income was the only money coming into the house, although I presume that there was some kind of sickness benefit payment for my grandfather and that their 'real' daughter, my birth-mother Eileen, and her husband helped out financially on a regular basis.

Beyond money, there was one legacy which my grandfather passed to me while I was still in junior school and which has had a value greater than anything else in my later life: he taught me to stand up for myself, to be independent and strong and not let anybody push me around.

Those were valuable assets, I'm sure you'll agree, for anyone planning to become a dominatrix.

CHAPTER 6

SEXUAL AWAKENING

It was the chilly touch of colder air on the skin of my bare legs that aroused me from the depths of my early-hours-of-the-morning sleep. Then just 11 years old, I could sleep for England, and so I was still barely conscious as I felt the weight of the bedcovers slowly lift from my thighs. I was certain, at first, I was dreaming, albeit a somewhat sexual dream for such a little girl. Perhaps the then love of my life, Tom Cruise, had decided to pop in to the bedroom and make all my pre-pubescent dreams come true? The Hollywood actor was much on my mind at that age. I was enjoying a sleepover at a schoolfriend's house and we had been giggling all evening about how much we would all love to kiss him. As I came fully awake, however, I realised that someone – most certainly not the infinitely desirable Mr Cruise – was gradually drawing the sheets off my half-naked body. I shot bolt upright in bed, barely stifled a scream and came face to face in the dark of the bedroom with my friend's father, crouching at the end of the bed and peering intently down at the schoolgirl white pants which were pretty much all that now covered my body. Chaos was about to ensue.

The year was 1985 and the evening had started as one of the most giggly, fun times I had enjoyed for a while. In the long summer holidays I had agreed to go and stay at a friend's house for a sleepover party with two other girls. None of us were yet at an age to be sexually active but all of us were besotted with celebrity idols in a way that only young girls can truly understand. My passion then (as now, if truth be told) was for the actor Tom Cruise who had just shot to sexy stardom in the film *Risky Business* and whose forthcoming role as a raunchy Sex God in the movie *Top Gun* was already being trailed in teen magazines and television shows. I loved Tom with a passion and had spent a good part of the evening proving my devotion by engaging in a kissing contest, competing against the smooching abilities of my equally-besotted friend. The game was simple: we each had a photograph of Tom Cruise and the winner would be the one who could kiss his image for the longest time. It truly was 'no contest' and I think I can still claim that 21 minutes is the world-record for 'Cruise-kissing' if such an achievement ever enters the record books.

The competition in my friend's bedroom was followed by all of us sharing a whispered, graphic account of what we thought we might do to attract Tom's interest were he to stroll in through the bedroom door. We none of us knew much about sex but could all imagine a few of the sexy delights we might offer him. (With the experience I've since gained in the adult industry, I could offer him an even better time now, should he ever wish to take up the offer.)

With Tom's, lip-dampened photographs safely put away for the night, all three of us had settled down to sleep on a couple of mattresses spread out across the bedroom floor. The house was already quiet: my friend's mother had gone to bed and her father was in the habit of staying up alone until the early hours downstairs. I snuggled down under the sheets in the middle of the group and, with our bedtime much later than usual, we must all have fallen quickly off to sleep. I don't really have any idea of what time I woke up, but I was conscious of this sudden, freezing cold sensation on my legs; it was utterly ice cold. I woke up with a thudding heart, which is a bizarre experience to have, and was aware of someone else in the room. I was wearing just a short nightshirt and knickers and, kneeling at the end of the bed, lifting up the hem of my nightie and staring intently at my pants, was my friend's dad, Ian. Even more disturbingly, he was wearing nothing except his underpants.

He looked more terrified than me when I spun around and saw him. He was mouthing the words 'sorry, sorry, really sorry' as he jumped up and sped out through the bedroom door and off down the stairs. By then I was screaming; it was such a shock and it took me a moment to realise that he must have been looking under the covers for a while before he disturbed me by actually touching my clothes. With my friends now awake and asking what had happened, my would-be voyeur's wife came sleepily into the room.

'He was going to touch me, he was going to do something to me,' I gasped.

53

'What on earth do you mean? Touch you? Who was touching you?'

'Ian. He was lifting the quilt up and looking at me; he was looking at my pants, he was going to do something...'

The words tumbled out in a jumble because I was truly upset and frightened. It was the first time that I had ever thought that somebody was going to touch me like that. It dawned on me that I could have been raped and I was shaking with fear. My friend's mum looked shocked and called downstairs to her husband: 'Ian, Ian, come upstairs would you?'

He wandered in to the room as cool as a cucumber, and by now fully dressed. 'What? What's going on, what's the matter?' he asked, his face all puzzled innocence. He listened, and did a good job of appearing to be horrified, as his wife explained that I was 'making accusations' that he had been in the bedroom.

'But I've just been downstairs watching the telly,' he protested. 'What's she on about?' And then he turned directly to me, still cowering under the bedclothes: 'What are you talking about; I haven't been near you.'

Faced with a blatant lie, I pleaded to be believed: 'But he was here, honest... he was just wearing his pants.'

'What colour pants did he have on?' asked his wife.

'Black... he was wearing black pants and nothing else at all.'

'Well, that's odd because he doesn't have any black pants anyway. You must have been dreaming. You've let your imagination run away with you. It's naughty to say such things... Now let's say no more about it and get you all back to sleep.'

I was pretty sure that his wife believed me about what had happened but had decided to protect her own family, whatever the truth of the matter. Then the guy's daughter also joined in the attack. 'It's all that Tom Cruise stuff, isn't it?' she declared. 'We've been talking about kissing him and then you must have dreamed it and blamed my dad!'

'No... I'm telling you, I'm telling you... he was in the room and looking at me.'

'Well my dad wouldn't do that. And we were here on either side of you and I didn't feel anything.'

And that was that. I was left, basically, accused of being a liar and nothing more was mentioned about the incident. I knew I hadn't imagined what had happened but, in the face of such united family resistance, I had no way of proving it. My last thought as I finally drifted back to sleep was that it had been dark in the room and perhaps those pants had been blue, not black.

That was the end of my summer trips to stay with my friend. Although I had spent lots of time there in the past I never stayed in that house again. Nobody said a word about the covers that had moved in the night-time, the incident was never mentioned in any way, but I was never invited again. I wanted to tell my grandmother about it but I thought, 'his wife doesn't believe me, his daughters don't believe me, why should anyone else believe me?' Not long afterwards, however, the next time I saw my biological mother, I told her the story of what had happened and why I was no longer staying with my friend. I was still angry and upset that nobody had done anything about it.

'I believe you Miranda,' my mother said, 'but don't tell your grandmother, she won't understand how anyone could do that and it will upset her dreadfully.'

My mother said that my story had not come as a surprise: 'I know the family and I know him, he's a creep and he's tried it on with women before. I know one woman who was pinned up against the wall in their kitchen and had to fight him off.'

It was yet a further shock to me that she could have been so naïve. I was shocked that my mother had never warned me of the dangers I could face, even though she knew some of that family's history and that I had stayed there often in the past.

Looking back now at what happened, I think my fears of rape and sexual assault were probably an over-reaction. Knowing men better as I do now, I guess that the guy was little more than a frustrated voyeur and that he would have been unlikely to do more than look whilst two other girls slept in the same bed and his wife was next door. But it was hardly conducive to making me trust the adults in my life. Not long afterwards I was to lose my virginity to another predatory adult – in fact to two predatory adults, twice my age, in the same sexual adventure… on the same afternoon.

CHAPTER 7

SEX EDUCATION

It is perhaps unsurprising that I never received any form of sex education, or information about my own sexual development, from my grandparents because, although I did not realise it at the time, they were of a different, older generation who found it deeply embarrassing to talk about sex in any shape or form. In our house, if anything remotely sexual ever came on the television, there would be a muttered word or two such as, 'We don't want this nonsense, do we?' and channels would be switched as fast as my granddad could find the remote control. That meant that I was fast approaching my teenage years with little more than playground gossip to prepare me for the emotional and physical changes that were beginning to affect my body. I had, of course, picked up a pretty good idea of the general mechanics of reproduction from friends and the occasional television glimpse when parents were out of the room, but it was certainly never explained in any authoritative way.

What I did get from my grandparents was a subtle, though continual, pressure to avoid any possibility of teenage pregnancy; hardly surprising when you consider what had happened to their own 15-year-old daughter not so many years before. Nothing was ever said directly but the thought was always there. I must be careful not to have a child as my mother had done. The message was drummed in by implications with small comments such as, 'You know you have to get your education Miranda' or 'You've got to go to university to do well. You want to live your life to the full, perhaps go travelling before you settle down.' The idea that I must do well at school and get qualified with a good education was a constant theme.

I suppose my earliest grasp of the fact that there were distinct differences between the sexual equipment of boys and girls came in my first days at school. I remember at the age of six or seven playing childish games of 'doctors and nurses' with friends in the more secluded areas of the playground; all variations of some kind on the age-old children's curiosity of 'show me yours and I'll show you mine'. It was all very innocent, and all a far cry from the sort of grown-up doctors and nurses games I play with my clients these days. Ironically, given the fact that I now spend much of my time with people stripping their clothes off in front of me, as a child I was always the one who hung back and never, never, volunteered for the 'I'll show you mine' part of the equation. I was far too shy and retiring to have even considered pulling my pants down. I was far more the type who would stand quietly at the back and observe.

When I was about eight years old there was one girl who had older brothers and sisters and who was, for a while, thought to be the fount of all knowledge about sex. Her brothers had clearly gone out of their way to share all of the intricate details of human sexual reproduction. 'You have to have two boys and one girl and they put the girl on their shoulders and shake her around a lot and this green stuff comes out and you have a baby,' she explained one day to a group of us, all eager to learn of the hidden delights of romantic love. Even at that age I knew that this explanation differed somewhat from the accepted wisdom of our playground, but looking around at the other girls I could see that several of them were worrying that her version might just be the correct one.

It was at the sort of childish age where you see people kissing on television and immediately start to cringe; you are curious but it all seems a bit revolting to contemplate. I think I knew enough to find the whole idea of the vigorous shoulder-shaking rather amusing, but none of what I knew had ever been verified by a teacher or any other adult. I did talk about what the girl had said with my friend, Jennifer, and she agreed with me that it was complete nonsense. She told me that she talked about sex often with her parents and was surprised that I had never asked my mummy about it. 'You should ask her where babies come from,' she said. The thought of doing that was so alien to me that I never even contemplated following her advice. It was not until several years later, long after I had lost my virginity, that I ever had such a conversation with my grandmother. Purely being mischievous, and already knowing the answer, I posed the classic question: 'Mum, where do babies come from?'

'Well, it's the husband planting a seed... and then it grows...' was the hesitant reply.

'Like in a cabbage patch,' I ventured, trying desperately not to laugh.

'No, no, not really like that. I'm sure they will tell you all about it at school soon.'

I was fast approaching my teens, knowing most of the mechanics of sex but nothing of the emotional turmoil it might bring. With our lack of communication about the subject, my grandmother had never even mentioned the concept of periods to me, although I knew that I would one day start them because there were already girls in my class at Middle School who were having them. Then my best friend Jennifer came on with her periods before me and, in probably more detail than I might have wanted, insisted on telling me all about it.

My own periods started when I was 12, in the holidays between leaving Middle School and starting at High School. I remember I was wearing blue fishnet tights under a denim skirt and had been shopping with my grandmother. When I got home I discovered I was bleeding but, of course, I had no pad or tampons to use. I talked to my grandmother who had nothing for me either. 'Isn't that odd,' she said, 'I was thinking today when we were out that I should have bought something for you because you would be due around this sort of age, but I didn't actually get anything at all.' That was not actually much help to me at the time but my ever-resourceful grandmother made up a kind of pad out of cotton wool and gauze and then bought me proper pads after that.

And so I celebrated my thirteenth birthday knowing little more than I had picked up in playground gossip. I was vaguely interested in boys and I think I must, by then, have discovered masturbation. It was a secret pleasure to be enjoyed under the bedclothes at night and increasingly often in the morning before dragging myself out of bed to face another day at school. My day-to-day life, however, was still largely devoted to the twin pursuits of coping with becoming a teenager and with sport at school.

Unfortunately for my moral welfare, the same could never have been said about my best friend Jennifer. Although still a virgin, Jennifer was crazy about sex and boys, any boy, of any shape or size or age. Now, don't get me wrong, I too was curious about boys but just not on the same industrial scale as Jennifer. I used to spend a lot of my time at her home because both her parents worked and we would often have the run of the house before they got back in the evening. She could always get into her parents' bedroom and I was soon introduced to her father's collection of soft-porn girlie magazines. More intrusively still, Jennifer would delight in peeking through her mother's wardrobe and showing me her 'kinky underwear'. We would sometimes dress up in them and show off in front of the bedroom mirror. They were all rather innocent, Anne Summers-type outfits rather than seriously kinky fetish wear but it seemed terribly naughty at the time. It was certainly hard to imagine my much older 'mother' buying anything remotely like that.

It was sometimes hard to get Jennifer to think or talk about anything else other than boys and so there was certain inevitability about what was to happen next. My friend's voracious appetite for meeting men, and my naïve willingness to follow, led us both into danger one day.

We regularly played a game after school in which we would head for the local shops and straightaway hitch up our school uniform skirts shorter and shorter. The game was to see how many car drivers would beep their horns and how many men might try to chat us up on the way. I loved the attention and was every bit as keen as Jennifer, but we were both about to learn a valuable lesson: that you can take such teasing too far. On one sunny afternoon, we were walking to the local shops as usual and happily collecting our requisite quota of 'beeps' from the passing cars. Suddenly one vehicle pulled into the side of the road right in front of us. A young Asian guy got out and stood smiling in front of us. I could see a couple of older men in the back of the car.

Smiling and friendly, this young Asian lad came out with a line which, even then to our 13-year-old ears, sounded as corny as hell.

'My dog's just had some really cute puppies,' he said. 'Do you want to come and have a look at them?'

'No thanks,' I said. 'Thanks, but no thanks.'

'Oh come on. We only live up the road. Where are you two from? Come on and have a look, you'll love them.'

The more both of us said we weren't interested, the more persistent he became. He was chatting, chatting, chatting but I ended up just repeating: 'No, no I'm not interested.' While Jennifer finally said, 'No I'm not going to see them, I've got puppies at home,' and took a step back.

'Come on Jennifer,' I said, 'let's go.'

With no warning he suddenly grabbed me around the middle and tried to drag me to the car. I was too shocked to scream but I was wriggling and fighting like mad. He might have succeeded in forcing me in through the open door but then Jennifer grabbed me and started pulling me away. He got hold of Jennifer too but by then I had hold of the fence and nothing was going to make me let go. Even at that age I was strong and wiry from all the sports I played at school, and I was hanging on for dear life.

We were both screaming, 'Get off... get off us' and the guys still sitting in the car were shouting 'Come on, come on, get her in quick'. It was total chaos and getting noisier by the second but, amazingly, no other cars or pedestrians stopped to come to our aid. In the end our attacker realised that his friends were not going to help and, without them, he wasn't going to win. He swore wildly at me, released his grip and jumped into the car as it sped off.

It had been the closest of calls, we were both shaking with the shock but thankfully we were both unharmed. We had not walked far from our school gates and there was a payphone right there so we decided to call the police. We had the car registration number and knew exactly what the guys had looked like, especially the younger one who had been the most dangerous. It was the one and only time that I have had to dial 999, and it was a complete waste of time: nobody answered the emergency call. Hardly able to believe it, I dialled the operator and blurted out that I needed to speak to the police. There was a short pause and then the operator was apologising profusely: 'I'm sorry caller, I just cannot get a reply from the police service.' In the confusion that followed, the operator offered to take down our details: 'I'll get someone to contact you as soon as I can.' The last thing that Jennifer and I wanted, however, was to have the police turning up on our doorsteps: my parents would never have let us out again! I instantly hung up the phone and we hurried back home. To this day I regret that my emergency call was not answered. That young guy had been determined to get us into that car, his older friends had been anxious to get their hands on us, and I just hope that nothing ever happened to other women because they were not caught that day. The attempted abduction should have been salutary lesson to Jennifer and me but at the age of 13 we all believe we are untouchable and immortal.

And at 13, I was only really interested in the opposite sex in a 'I ought to get a boyfriend' sort of way but my friend's obsession with sex – and my childish willingness to go along with her – were soon to cost us both our virginity.

CHAPTER 8

LOSING MY VIRGINITY

On one of the many afternoons when she spurned getting the bus in order to walk home from school, Jennifer had met a man more than twice her age whom she felt was a promising candidate to take her unwanted virginity. She told me all about him the following morning at school: 'Oh Miranda, he's great. He's called Ron, he's 26 and he wants to see me again – and he's got a friend, and he really wants to meet you too.' The age of Jennifer's latest conquest might perhaps have set alarm bells ringing in my mind but I was well-used to her chatting up every man – in fact *any* man – with whom she came into contact. It was after all the whole purpose of our regular strolls through West London with our school skirts hitched high on our thighs. 'Oh come on Miranda, it'll be fun; he's good-looking and his friend really wants to see you and you have to come with me.'

Despite some initial reservations I agreed, as I always did, to go along with Jennifer's plan. We set off after classes to meet her new man and his 'friend' who had clearly been earmarked for me. Although Jennifer was the one who always did all of the talking, we both knew that I was the one to whom most of the men were attracted. It was therefore nothing out of the ordinary for Jennifer's guy, Ron, to start chatting me up as soon as we met. It did not upset Jennifer at all; she was equally happy getting to know his friend and I was pleasantly surprised by Ron's good looks.

It was a rainy afternoon when we all met outside Ron's parents' house, a mile or two from my school. It seemed only natural to accept the boys' invitation to 'come into the garage to get out of the rain'. What was perhaps not quite so natural was that two mattresses had been laid out on the garage floor with a few blankets to transform them into useable, if temporary, beds. There was, as you will already have guessed, a certain inevitability about what was to happen over the next half-hour. Ron was kissing me and his friend was kissing Jennifer and things just rolled along a little bit too quickly for me to think. I lay down on the bed with Ron and didn't really resist when he started stroking my body. Boys had touched me before but not quite in the urgent and intimate way he was touching me now. I can't pretend that I was enthralled by what was happening but I went along with it willingly enough. It all just sort of happened, really.

Looking back on the events of that afternoon, it is obvious that those two 26-year-olds had planned all along to seduce us with the minimum of fuss and effort. Being half their age, both virgins and still at school we must have been the easiest of targets. The only thing that might have given me pause for thought was if they had not used 'protection'. The story of my own birth-mother's pregnancy from her first sexual encounter was always in my mind. But Ron and his friend had each come prepared with condoms and that was never an issue.

The precise details of this distinctly unromantic tryst are now a little hazy. The lights were on in the garage but Jennifer and I were both lying under blankets. I was still wearing most of my school uniform and worried that it was getting damp and creased. I certainly remember being self-conscious about my body as Ron fumbled his way inside my clothes while continuing to smother me with kisses. I don't think he even undressed me completely, just unbuttoning my white school blouse, lifting my skirt up and pulling off my pants.

There was the briefest of pauses in his attentions as he slipped a condom on under the blanket and I was aware that Jennifer was lying a few feet away. Her guy was by now on top of her and she was making all of the correct 'Ooh-ah... I am *really* enjoying this' sort of noises. A few moments later I was conscious of a tight, painful sensation as Ron entered me and started rocking backwards and forwards. I think I made a few 'Ooh ah' noises as well, although the truth is that I was thinking: 'Oh God, this isn't really very nice at all. It's bloody uncomfortable. If this is what it is all about, I am not interested anymore.' In common, I believe, with many women's own experiences, the most charitable thing I can say about my first fuck was that it didn't last very long. Ron seemed to come very quickly.

I received a few slightly more perfunctory kisses as Ron rolled off of me and lay for a moment under the blanket. The others had clearly finished as well and I could hear Jennifer giggling and muttering with her man. It didn't seem at all unnatural when one of the guys suddenly suggested, 'Let's swap.' Clearly having planned the move all along, the two men quickly changed beds and partners and I found myself now kissing the friend who had always been intended for me from the start. He was a nice enough looking guy as well and accepting him was presumably part of the deal. I did not raise any objection the second time around, even though the sex was now a distinctly painful activity which I just hoped would be over as rapidly as it had been with Ron. One quick condom application later, a few more uncomfortable thrusts, and my daily double of losing my virginity to two men in the same afternoon was complete.

The same cannot be said of my poor friend Jennifer. I knew that she really liked Ron but he was clearly having problems. Jennifer was disappointed that Ron could not get erect enough to have sex with her as well. 'She's killed my dick… she's killed my dick,' he kept saying, presumably needing to use my virginal tightness as an excuse for his own erectile problems with Jennifer.

Despite her disappointment in not arousing Ron enough to perform his manly duties, Jennifer was delighted to have lost her virginity. The footballers' cliché 'over the moon' best describes her mood as we continued our interrupted walk home. 'We're women now,' she said several times. Jennifer asked me how I was feeling. 'Sore,' I replied, 'and worried we're not going to get home in time for our 7.30pm curfew; and then I'm in trouble with my mum.' After what had happened that afternoon, my need to get home at the time my grandparents had demanded perhaps illustrates the pointlessness of such parental restrictions. The truth is, however, that I was undoubtedly a little shell-shocked by what had happened. I hadn't had the slightest inkling when I agreed to meet the guys that such a thing was going to happen that day. Now that it had happened I think I was emotionally a little numb. I certainly was not physically numb because I remember sitting at school the next day and being worried that I was still so very uncomfortable between my legs. It had not been a nice experience, nothing like as pleasurable as I had imagined and I wasn't overly anxious to try it again.

Even so, and to my shame, it wasn't long before my still-tender vagina was called into action again. Just three days later, on a Saturday, Jennifer was chasing a boy far nearer to our own age and I was drafted in as usual to make up a double date with his friend. Once again, however, the plan went slightly awry because I ended up with Trevor, Jennifer's original target and she started dating his friend Mark. With the cast list sorted to my satisfaction we spent the afternoon wandering around the shops and a local park with the boys on the look-out for somewhere to take us a little more intimate than the town centre. Eventually the guys resorted to drastic measures. They broke into a disused water tower and led us upstairs to a room that although mostly bare concrete and industrial pipes was at least warm and dry. Judging by the debris scattered around, others must have been dossing there in the recent past and probably using drugs. Unlike the first occasion with Ron, I now knew what was likely to happen and the naughtiness of these new, different surroundings made me excited in a way I certainly had not been before.

Trevor and I ended up having sex while Jennifer had her evil way with Mark on the other side of the room. The game was nothing like as painful as it had been a few days earlier; I think my body had sort of recovered from that agony, but again to me it wasn't really an enjoyable experience. Not as traumatic as the first time but I kind of felt that it was one of those things that guys want to do and that therefore I needed to get it out of the way as soon as possible and get on with other things. I do remember being in the missionary position on the rather hard floor and being grateful that it was once again certainly not a marathon session of sex.

Even though the earth had hardy moved for either of us, Trevor was keen enough to ask me out for another date and we were boyfriend and girlfriend for a while. He lived just a short bus ride away from my grandparents' home, and sex was regularly on the menu when I could slip away from the house and hop on the bus to his home. By then the sex had got better. As I was still barely 13 years old, my grandparents were constantly questioning where I was going and I constructed what I thought was a foolproof and elaborate web of lies to conceal my new and growing enthusiasm for outings after school. The best and most obvious excuse was that I was simply seeing Jennifer, but she was now regularly shagging Mark, and the times of our dates sometimes failed to coincide.

My strict 7.30 curfew was broken more and more often as I found it harder to tear myself away from the fun of my boyfriend's bed, and my grandparents started digging a little deeper into my life. Once they realised that my Jennifer excuse was holed below the waterline, my next line of defence was to invent fictitious evenings with another 'friend from school'. The Asian girl I claimed to be visiting did exist but we certainly were never friends. I had grasped at her name as a drowning man grasps at a straw but I am sure that her parents would have been baffled to learn that I was allegedly a frequent visitor to their house, a home that in reality I had never even seen. Amazingly, my grandmother trustingly accepted my tale… for a while.

My downfall came because I had never counted on my grandmother sharing quite as much of my life as she did do with her daughter, my missing biological mother, who then lived more than 30 miles away with her husband and growing young family. My birth-mother had always stayed as part of my life, visiting me at my grandparents' home or having me visit her when I stayed with my aunt nearby. There had been lots of toys and presents and clothes from her through the years but the relationship had been far more strained ever since I had discovered the truth about my birth.

Now, unbeknown to me, the 'mum' who I lived with was sharing her worries about my late nights and suspect behaviour with my birth-mum, a younger woman who represented a much more daunting prospect when it came to lying through my teeth. The first I knew of her growing involvement was a visit in which she suggested we go for a walk together to the local shops. En route I found myself being cross-questioned at length by a woman who was far harder to fool than my adoptive parents.

'So what's this girl's name?' she asked chattily. 'Oh and where does she live… which road is that… what is her address… what's her mum like… does she have many brothers and sister for you to play with…?' The questions poured out in a torrent that I was ill-equipped to dam or divert. For a while I struggled to maintain the pretence of my Asian friend but I knew too few real facts to fool anyone. 'I think it's a good idea of I meet this girl's mum, don't you?' my birth-mother said. 'Shall I give her a call?'

It was a killer blow and red-faced and stammering I blurted out that I had told a 'little fib' to my grandmother. That little fib was soon exposed as a series of whopping great lies as I finally admitted that I was seeing a boy and that my clandestine visits to his home each evening were the reason for breaking my curfew. I had been well and truly caught out – but I knew that however tough the questioning, one fact must remain a tight-lipped secret.

'I'm worried, are you having sex with this boy?' my birth-mother demanded, a question that would never have passed my grandmother's lips.

'No, of course, I'm not… he's not like that.'

'Well you know it's against the law, don't you? You can get done for that at your age, and so can the boy. If the police catch you you'll be in trouble.'

The prospect of PC Plod peeking through the curtains to spy on me every time I dropped my knickers was worrying, but seemed to be a little unlikely. More worrying was my family's joint insistence that in future they would need to safeguard my welfare more closely. 'We need to keep tabs on you a little more,' my birth-mother insisted. 'You should hold on to your virginity until you meet someone special, the man you'll marry.' I was the only one among those in the room who knew that her concern was a little late in arriving: quite a while too late.

The end result of the 'fibs' debacle was that I was grounded for weeks by the combined forces of my grandmother and my birth-mother working in harmony to ensure my moral welfare. I was not allowed to go out anywhere other than to school and back, and my relationship with Trevor was stopped in its tracks. Demonstrating the true spirit of schoolgirl friendship, Jennifer took the opportunity to start going out with him herself. As soon as she mentioned that she had 'seen' Trevor the evening before I knew beyond a shadow of doubt that they must have had sex. I didn't really mind because I was imprisoned in my nan's house anyway. It did feel a little unfair when she revealed that my former boyfriend had been grading my performance: 'He says you've got a ten out of ten body, but a six out of ten face,' she announced with some glee.

So after the briefest of outings, my burgeoning sexual history had pretty much ground to a halt. A one-afternoon stand with two older men who took my virginity had been followed by a few inexpert couplings with a lad more my own age. None of the above had been much to write home about and none of it had been enjoyable enough to encourage me to seek sex elsewhere. I suppose that my reluctance to repeat the experience was some sign of how well my grandparents had succeeded in instilling at least some sense of morality throughout my childhood. I could not have articulated it at the time but I knew that something was not quite right about mere random sexual encounters. I did feel that I wanted a boyfriend but knew in my heart that I should be having sex with a proper partner, rather than with strangers to whom I had barely even spoken. No such standards had ever been spelled out directly at home but the message had been repeatedly conveyed by implication. It was a drip-drip, almost subliminal feed of my grandparents' morality: 'You do not have sex until you are married; look what happened to your mother at such a young age; be careful, be a good girl, behave.' My grandparents had never had that sex education talk with me, but clearly something of their message had stuck in my mind.

Perhaps more importantly, I was also spending a lot less time at that stage with my sex-mad friend Jennifer. Without her around to chat up a seemingly endless string of would-be partners, I was happy to concentrate on my schoolwork and to try and solve my perennial problem of never having any money. The age-limit for working in a 'Saturday' job was supposed to be 15, but for a long time I had looked older than my age. It was easy enough to get a job as a waitress in a local café, the first of a string of dull jobs which served one purpose for me better than any other: they made me determined to get a good education, good qualifications in order that I would never again get stuck in that type of boring, dead-end job.

I was around 13 years old when I started my first waitressing job. The wages were about £10 each Saturday but that could rise by another pound or two if the customers contributed to my tips jar. The money felt like a fortune to somebody who had never been given more than £1 a week pocket money throughout their childhood. I can remember with crystal clarity how I spent my first week's wages. I bought a denim dress from a clothes shop just around the corner from the café. It was a fantastic sensation. 'Wow,' I thought, 'I can actually buy my own clothes. How cool is that.' Although I didn't know it at the time, the stretchy, tight, denim dress would prove to be an excellent investment. The following Saturday I wore it to work in the café. There was one customer who was like, 'Wow, you look amazing.' He was seriously chatting me up and making a continuous string of lurid comments suggesting that if I bent over just a little bit further in my short dress then I might show off my knickers. He was much older than me, a dirty, horrid old man – but he kept on giving my tips for my jar. Consequently I just smiled it off every time he called me over: 'Oh, just bend over here would you, and do this, pick this up for me.' I found him obnoxious but he kept making a point of showing me that he was dropping a pound here or there in my jar, which I instantly grabbed back and slipped into my pocket. I also made a point of never quite bending low enough to give him the reward he was seeking. It was an early lesson in handling men: always leave the customer wanting more.

Not all of the customers were as horrible as that guy but I did learn that there are some rude people, really incredibly rude people in this world. Waitressing was hard but I had plans for my wages. There had been a disaster at home and I knew exactly how that money was going to be put to good use. My nan had broken her Hoover. Unable to afford another, she had been struggling for months to keep the house clean with a tiny, manual carpet sweeper. That was the reason I saved up my earnings for the next two months. I know it may not now seem like a brilliant present but I was finally able to take my £80 and buy a vacuum cleaner in Argos. I carted it all the way back home on the bus and gave it to my nan for her birthday. It's one of my happiest teenage memories: 'She's brought me a Hoover; I've got a Hoover again,' she called out to my granddad. There actually were tears in her eyes and I knew she could not have been happier if I had purchased a Cartier diamond necklace. I thought 'Oh bless...' as she insisted on plugging it in that moment in order to vacuum every carpet in the house from top to bottom. The downside was that my granddad and I had to endure hours of multiple-cleaning with her popping in and out of each room, muttering to herself over the sound of the vacuum cleaner: 'This is so wonderful, wonderful; she's bought me a Hoover.'

My work in the café had served me – and the preternatural cleanliness of my grandmother's home – well. It did feel, however, that it was time to move on to a Saturday job that might be a fraction more interesting. I found another opportunity locally that offered slightly better wages and the chance to stay serving *behind* a counter rather than mixing in with the frequently obnoxious and ungrateful customers. The only trouble was that accepting this particular summer job meant facing up to my only serious fear in life.

I have a confession to make: 'My name is Miranda – I am a secret spheksophobic.' I have a morbid fear of wasps.

Now, every good dominatrix loves uncovering a client's secret phobias, their deep-seated fears that one can exploit to weaken their will, bend them to their knees and generally scare them half to death. Facing one's fears is a major part of why my clients come to visit me in the first place. They may outwardly be asking for a spanking, a caning, public humiliation and degradation, or to be wrapped up in multiple layers of latex: inwardly they are unknowingly facing their innermost, and most secret, fears. I always think that when a man or a woman confesses they are claustrophobic, for example, that a spell in my dungeon 'coffin box' will suit them just fine. It is a person-sized box in which I may bind you immovably, with multiple leather straps securing your wrists, forearms, ankles, calves, thighs, tummy, chest and forehead tight to the wall. When the coffin lid closes shut, just inches from your face, you are unable to move a muscle, unable to see through the inky blackness and even the sound of the outside world will be muffled. How long I leave you in that state depends on me. The skill, of course, which I have honed to a fine art over the years, is to know precisely when your rising terror is almost, but not quite, at the point of true panic. The whimpers you make, the sound of your breathing speeding up, the note of desperation in your voice all tell me precisely when you have suffered enough to have pumped-up adrenaline levels and your sexual desires to the max, whilst leaving you (just) on the right side of sanity.

Having praised the therapeutic benefits of facing one's fear, it will surprise you not one jot to know that I would not possibly follow my own advice and face up to my own phobia: spheksophobia... the fear of wasps. Given my total terror of having wasps anywhere near me, it was perhaps not the wisest move to accept my new job in a baker's shop. Attracted by the ever-present scent of jam doughnuts and cream cakes, the shop was wasp central station throughout the summer months. I was paranoid about being stung and once fled from the shop, abandoning an open till full of money rather than face up to a massive wasp that had chased me round the room. We are talking about a *big* wasp here; so large it could hardly fly... a doodlebug of an insect, probably a hornet, and maybe worse!

It is never easy to understand where such irrational fears

77

come from but I do remember one childhood incident which may have been to blame for turning me into a manic wasp-a-phobe. I was perhaps five years old when I saw a young girl in the playground who had two wasps caught up in her long blonde hair. She was screaming and slapping her hair trying to stop them buzzing round her ears and everyone – especially me – was too scared to help her. I can remember thinking, 'Oh God, thank God that isn't me.' No way on earth could I have helped her. The connection is that my reaction now to wasps follows a similar pattern. I throw up my hands to cover my ears and look around for something with which to cut off my hair if it flies in my direction. Better to have a rough and ready urchin haircut than a wasp in my ear.

CHAPTER 9

'A GOOD EDUCATION...'

From an early age, my loving grandfather drummed into me the importance of a 'good education'.

A highly intelligent man, Granddad was of a generation for whom a university education was outside of their wildest dreams. Instead he had left school early, joined the Navy and had later worked in a frustratingly modest job at a West London factory. Finally, ill-health forced him into premature retirement and led to a life in which we all existed on State benefits and the tiny sum my grandmother earned as a school dinner-lady. Perhaps spurred on by the way that good schooling had been denied to him, he was determined that I should not suffer the same fate. 'A *good* education Miranda,' he would tell me. 'You must get a good education. That's what will get you a good job, good money and a good life. Get a good education.'

With his words ringing in my ears, it was I who selected an all-girls' school for my secondary education. It may appear to be a decision more mature than my years might allow, but I was already aware that schools differed in their respective performances and also that girls almost always do better when the distraction of boys is removed from the educational equation. My home was just a few hundred yards from a mixed High School to which all of my friends were going; you could literally look out of our front door and see the school gates. I knew, however, that it was not a particularly high-achieving school. That knowledge came not from some in-depth study of educational league tables but from far more down-to-earth data – my grandmother worked there, and she didn't rate it at all.

My chosen alternative was much further away in Acton, the more highly-regarded Ellen Wilkinson School for Girls. Getting there involved a lengthy bus ride and then a walk of more than a mile but I knew it was the only way of keeping the faith with my granddad's dream. I never quite gathered who Ellen Wilkinson was but I did know her school was my best shot at that all important good education.

I always did well at school and working at weekends and in school holidays didn't stop my progress in the classroom. I could perhaps have done better, but life was always so busy with work and sport that I found I could leave exam preparation to the last moment and still pass with flying colours. Even for subjects such as English Literature, I would often get by without ever reading the books we were supposed to be studying. I would pick up instant study guides and flip through the summaries they provided, gleaning enough information to fake my way through the required essays and discussions. The one area that I could never fake, then or now, was my inability to spell. Often the simplest words can leave me stumped. The problem was that my teachers put all of the emphasis on skills such as being able to structure an essay and took no account of spelling. I would get top marks for an essay and receive the comment 'obviously the spelling needs more work', but I was never marked down for that weakness. On top of that I was always bursting with ideas that I wanted to get down on paper and I would write 20 pages when other kids were writing two. That sort of urgency leaves no time for proof-reading or worrying if one's handwriting can even be deciphered.

My other problem in gaining the education that I hoped would lead to a sparkling and fascinating career was the lack of parental support. My grandparents' tiny home, where I wrote on the kitchen table, was hardly made for undisturbed homework and my grandparents, deeply caring though they were, had no idea of how they might provide an environment conductive to study. Their lack of supportive skills was even more noticeable when it came to careers advice. I can remember saying to my grandmother: 'How do I know what job I should do and what courses there are? I don't know what to do.' She had no idea of how to help. She was a good dressmaker and had done menial cleaning work, so had not the faintest idea how to look for a job in an office. My grandparents' knowledge of the careers market came from jobs such as working in a shop or on the factory floor. They could never have guided me towards being a doctor or a lawyer or any profession like that. Yet when I look back, I bear no resentment: their lack of knowledge was their limitation, not a lack of willingness to help.

I could get slightly more guidance on the occasions when my birth-mother came to visit us. Knowing that other parents at the school often set their own children private homework, she would give me writing tasks to complete and sometimes we would talk about what career I might follow. But such advice was thinly spread and infrequently offered. In retrospect I can see that my life might have taken a very different direction if I had been raised by my younger birth-mother rather than by elderly grandparents. She could never have loved me more than they undoubtedly did, but perhaps my ambitions might have been channelled in other directions. And maybe the good things my grandparents gave me – a strong work ethic, a drive to succeed, a desire to make my own way in the world – would have been lost.

There is however one part of my teenage life that could have been very different if I had been raised by my mother rather than my grandmother. The larger than natural generation gap between me and my parents was having an effect. My unstoppable desire for increasing independence throughout my early teens was coming up against the immoveable object of my elderly grandparents' rules of behaviour. It was a clash beyond the normal generations: it could only lead to trouble.

CHAPTER 10

SPREADING MY WINGS

Just 13 years old, I was a tall girl for my age and even on my limited budget – and even though I say so myself – I looked pretty sexy when I was dressed up for a night on the town.

My closest friends and I easily got into clubs where the bouncers were more interested in the cleavage we were showing than in checking our IDs to ensure we were the requisite 18-plus. Distracting the doormen was not the reason I wore clubbing clothes revealing a lot more than they concealed, but it certainly helped at the entrance.

One favourite haunt was West London's biggest club, the famous Hammersmith Palais, sadly now demolished but in its time a great place for dancing. We rarely paid to get in because on many club nights entry was free before ten o'clock and we would slip in a few moments before the deadline, clutching handbags in which were hidden small bottles of gin, for me, and Pernod-and-Southern Comfort for Jennifer, still then my closest friend. The doormen were only really interested in searching the guys for anything dangerous, like knives. We had so few clothes on that they would have had trouble searching us anyway without being accused of indecent assault, so we invariably got away with our mini-smuggling operation. It meant that a few soft drink mixers were our only expense for the evening. Jennifer was always keen to get guys to buy us drink, but I was rarely interested in the men: I was there to drink and dance and, with the exception of the occasional kiss, I was always well behaved. The club had box-like, raised platforms on which you could dance and Jennifer and I would monopolise one of these for the night and dance our hearts out. One picture taken around that time shows me in tight black shorts and wearing a gold bum-bag: all the rage at the time. I'm not sure I was ever a great dancer but I just *loved* those nights, dancing for hours and eyeing up the talent, even if I was not particularly interested in the talent taking things any further.

In fact, I rarely got chatted up at the club nights. I immodestly thought I was the prettiest girl in the group but I must have been giving out 'I want to be alone' signals because I was so shy. I just got on with the dancing, fending off the occasional bad chat-up line from unattractive guys whom I would never have wanted to be with in a million years. I always seemed to attract the weird ones. I've been told many times since that I do have an 'unapproachable' air about me that deters men from trying to chat. If that's the case, it's ironic that I spend my days now surrounded by men who kneel at my feet, profess to worship the ground I walk on and constantly crave my attention. Perhaps 'treat them mean… keep them keen' really does work after all.

If you're going to do the job properly then clubbing takes a lot of energy and long, long hours late, late into the night – just the sort of energy levels we possess in our early teens. I was unstoppable when I was having fun. The downside, of course, was that dancing till the early hours isn't conducive to waking up bright and breezy for school in the morning. On top of that, at the age of 13 or 14, I was often trying to get home late at night from some pretty seedy parts of London and it is no surprise that my desire for independence was giving my elderly grandparents nightmares. The irony is that, at least at that age, I truly was not doing anything naughty on my nights out and they really could have slept easily in their beds. Both Nan and Granddad were however convinced that I must be meeting men and would undoubtedly end up being raped or worse – although I was never quite certain what the 'worse' might entail. It was a typical clash of the generations, with me testing their boundaries and my grandparents struggling constantly to rein me in. The only difference in this case was that the game had skipped a generation; where I should have been pushing against someone of my birth-mother's age, I was struggling against 'parents' of a generation once removed. It was a recipe for seemingly endless conflict and eventual disaster.

As my rows with Nan and Granddad escalated they began to despair of having any control over me. Looking back on it now, I must have been a nightmare for them. I was no longer listening to anything they said. I was rude, disrespectful, had a tendency to slam doors on my way up to my room where I would pump my music up loud in the certain knowledge that the noise would drive them crazy. I'm not proud of my behaviour then and I am so glad that when I had eventually matured enough to realise what a shit I had been, I was able to apologise to them before they died for putting them through the hell of my teenage years.

Through it all, as I think they always understood, I did carry on loving them. It was just that they were of such a different generation that their rules seemed stricter, their curfews earlier and their ideas more outdated than those of any of my friends' parents. Although I had long known that they were my adoptive parents, rather than my birth parents, I've never believed that was a deciding factor in our relationship; the related age gap that went with that situation seems to me to have been a more relevant concern. But, it may well have influenced the way that my grandparents thought of me and their responsibilities to bring me up as a decent girl who could be trusted to be safely in her bed each night rather than gallivanting around in clubs. Having willingly embraced the role of parents, could it be that they felt even more duty bound than 'real' parents to keep me safe?

Apart from the relatively harmless drinking, nothing happened on those club nights that would have worried my grandparents anyway if they had come along with me. But just on principle my nan worried incessantly about me being out with friends late at night. After endless rows that were getting us nowhere, my birth-mother and her husband got involved and actually tried to act as peacemakers. Her husband would sometimes drive over from their home, 30 miles or so outside London, and stay the night in order that he could pick me up from the club in his car and see me home safely. I think it was my birth-mother's attempt to help me, because she privately felt that my grandparents were just too strict about everything. But, having legally given me away to them in the adoption, she had no authority to control what I was or was not doing.

My case to be allowed to go out late was also helped by one particularly kind taxi-driver who would make a point of waiting for me and my best friend on club evenings. He refused other fares just to take us home and told us, 'I've got a daughter of my own and I want to know that she gets home safely.' He always undercharged us for the fare and had no ulterior motive of any kind for helping us: just a genuinely nice man.

For a while the compromises calmed down the situation between myself and my grandparents a little but the rows over my independence continued. Over the next 18 months, as I grew ever more determined to lead my own life, the arguments were scheduled to get worse – much, much worse.

CHAPTER 11

FIRST
LOVE

From my earliest teenage years, about the time I discovered that I could get really fun feelings in my ladybits if I wiggled my fingers in just the correct way, I grew more and more interested in all types of fetish imagery.

I think Madonna – the singer, not the religious icon – has a lot to answer for in turning a generation of young girls onto rubber, leather and conical bras. I was drawn to her music videos and to magazine images of her outfits. I found I was browsing through any newspaper stories that dealt with fetish items, whether they were on the fashion pages or from a sex story in the *News of the World*. It was clear that from this early age I was interested in such fetish material although I've never really thought to ask why. I'm not a reflective, self-analytical person in that way. I'm more the type who will think: 'Well that worked for me... now what else can I find?'

My own fashion sense was limited to what I could afford, which was never much, but from about the age of 13, I seemed to always be the girl wearing the shortest, tightest skirts in any group. My dress sense may have been outrageous but I was still shy and retiring and despite the occasional sexual foray, I was soon approaching my fifteenth birthday relatively chaste and certainly with no regular boyfriend. I knew I wanted to explore some of the sexually exciting fetish imagery I enjoyed, but had no one with whom I could play. Then I met my first love and my sex life exploded in all sorts of fascinating new directions.

Tom was 6 ft 2ins tall, dark-haired and must have inherited some of his good looks from his attractive mother. He was from a distinctly middle-class family, living in a posher part of West London. I fancied him like crazy from the moment I saw him. With that overwhelming passion of young love, I immediately thought, 'He's tall, brown-haired, stocky but fit, a nice guy from a nice family. This is the man I will spend the rest of my life with.'

Tom was the first guy I really fancied, as opposed to the few other guys I had slept with, where sex had just sort of happened with little thought or desire on my part. I met him through a friend who was going out with his brother and then spent an afternoon after school with him and some friends in his bedroom. Nothing happened between us but I was really impressed with the fact that he had proper graffiti sprayed all over the white walls and that he and his friends were smoking 'puff'. I think I had taken pills at clubs before but that was my introduction to any sort of drugs culture.

When I got to know the family better I learned that his parents had split and that since then his mother had rather lost control of her sons. It was odd because I remember thinking that they were from a middle-class background, in a posh house, and were spraying graffiti on their walls and using drugs whereas I was poor and from a council estate but would never had dreamt of behaving like that.

The afternoon we met up, everyone was chatting, although as usual I was the quiet one of the group. Before then I had never seen the Monty Python film *Life of Brian*, but one of Tom's friends put on the video and I found it utterly hilarious. Perhaps fuelled by the 'puff' we were all smoking I was in pain from laughing so much and I was getting on really well with Tom's friend, which didn't go down too well with him. The next time I saw him he left me in no doubt that, although he was again with a group of friends, I was the one in whom he was interested. I'm sure we must have had our first kiss that night, although I can remember very little about the evening because the guys took us to a pub and got me completely and utterly drunk. They were buying me gin and I just couldn't handle spirits like that. It was mortifying to go home with Tom and to have his mother find me pissed out of my mind. There was no way I could go home in that state and so she let me stay the night. It was my first night in my new boyfriend's house but any idea of naughty games was out of the question. I actually spent the entire night throwing up in their toilet and being looked after by his mother. By morning I just wanted to die.

It's an ill wind, however, that blows nobody good and there was to be a happy outcome from my out-of-character night of drunken behaviour. Tom's mum had telephoned my grandmother to explain that I wasn't really well enough to go home and that she was happy for me to stay in their spare bedroom. The next morning she drove me home and met my nan who was impressed by the fact she had a car and was totally reassured that I had been safe for the night. They swapped telephone numbers and Tom's mum said I would always be welcome to stay over at their house in the future. I was deeply ashamed and embarrassed by what had happened but it did mean that forever after that I could tell my grandparents I was staying at Tom's house and they believed me every time.

So Tom became my first love and we started exclusively dating each other. He went to the local all boys' school and I was at the girls' equivalent, so we took to travelling home on the bus together several nights a week and then mostly just hanging out in his room. I fancied him from the start and we started having sex almost immediately. The first time with him was in his own bed at his house while his mum was out at work. His grandmother lived with the family and she was in the house at the time but, luckily for us, was a bit deaf. For the first time I really enjoyed the sex and it became important and fun for me. From then onwards there was no holding us back.

I would see Tom several times a week and at weekends, sometimes staying the night and sometimes not. I had no worries about getting pregnant because I had been prescribed the pill a year earlier, not as a contraceptive, but as a treatment for my acne. It was a really effective acne cure and I ended up being prescribed three-monthly contraceptive injections for the same reason. They stopped my periods completely as well as removing the fear of an unwanted baby. With that freedom, a boy I really fancied and a bed where we could have plenty of privacy, I became something of a sex maniac. I could hardly keep my hands off of Tom's body and I was usually the instigator when we were going to have sex; my sex drive seemed to be extremely high because I liked him so much. As far as I can remember I did have orgasms through masturbation before I met Tom, but certainly not with any other men. Now I found I could come if I rode on top of him, although no other position worked in the same way for me. As a result I was always trying to arouse him so that I could, literally, jump on top of him in bed. It was a long time later that I realised that he was not the best-endowed man on the block, but in my relative innocence size truly didn't matter to me at that age. He was large enough to make me happy.

Even though I was the one doing the jumping, Tom enjoyed the sex just as much as I did. He was younger than me and I was also his first regular girlfriend. He always claimed that he wasn't a virgin when he met me but I think he was lying; I certainly told a few white lies of my own, assuring him that I had only ever had sex with one man before. I thought the truth of several different partners, including the two men who shared my virginity between them, might be too much for him to take. Given the regularity of our sex it's not surprising that we started to explore our own desires more and more and I was soon leading Tom into sexual areas that had always interested me.

Me being the one on top was our regular sexual position and it seemed only natural to pin his arms back against the bed as I rode him. It excited me enormously and he certainly didn't object. Then, because I was always the one taking the lead, I tied his hands to the bedhead. Since we both had started out wearing our school uniforms before various items were discarded as superfluous to requirements, it seemed only natural to use both our school ties as my very first pieces of bondage equipment. In time I got hold of some rope and I did try tying him up properly to the bed; looking back now I can see what a terrible bondage job I did, but we both enjoyed it at the time. I think that Tom was a little like a rabbit caught in the headlights: fascinated by what was rushing towards him and unable to move away. From there we graduated onto other domination experiments, always with me in charge of proceedings. One evening I brought some ice into the bedroom, blindfolded him and started rubbing it over his sensitive parts. He was going crazy underneath me, half enjoying the experience and half hating it. I just thought it was so interesting that he could still feel horny and excited despite the discomfort I was causing. It was perhaps the first time that I realised that I hugely enjoyed having power over another helpless human being. It's a power I've enjoyed ever since; a power to be used responsibly and, at times, tempered by kindness but it is a highly addictive feeling I love to this day. I suspected even then that I was a step ahead of my peers in my sexual activities but never felt guilty about it. They probably weren't tying their boyfriends to the bed but to me it felt like the most natural thing in the world.

As time went by, Tom and I grew bolder in arranging for me to stay the night in his bed. As far as my grandparents were concerned, Tom's mum was happy for me to stay over at her house in the spare room, as far as Tom's mother was concerned I was leaving most evenings to go home. The truth was that we were busily deceiving both of them. At the end of the evening I would say goodbye to Tom's family and he would then offer to walk me to the nearby bus stop. We knew that while we were out the whole family would go off to bed, making it easy for him to sneak me back into the house and upstairs to his bedroom. They were having work done to the house and so for a long while there was scaffolding around the building. That made it even easier for me to shimmy up the scaffold poles after I had supposedly left to go home and climb back in through the bedroom window. In the morning, I would simply leave by the same route whilst everyone was getting up and then a few minutes later turn up at the door to 'visit' Tom again. 'Morning, sleep well? Good to see you.'

In the end of course, I got caught out. I was so tired one morning that I let Tom go off to school on his own whilst I stayed put in his bed. I thought I had locked the door but his mother caught me out. It didn't go down too well to find me asleep in her son's bed, but the relationship had lasted for so long by then that she hardly made any fuss. The love affair with Tom had led to a temporary truce in my fights with my grandparents. But 18 months down the line, as with many first loves, cracks were starting to appear in our relationship. The end was nigh and the end of one relationship was to rekindle all of the problems in the relationship with my own family. The real war of independence was about to break out at home, and it was not going to end well.

CHAPTER 12

GOING OFF
THE RAILS

I knew Tom was lying when he told me he'd had a quiet weekend at home. I'd already heard that he and his mates had been to a local club and, in a way which was starting to typify our friendship, he hadn't wanted to take me along. He always said that having me with him on a night out meant that he couldn't 'relax' in the same way as if he was on his own. As far as I knew, Tom was not being unfaithful to me but a clear pattern was emerging. It seemed that I was good enough for him to use for sex during the week but at the weekends he wanted to go clubbing with his mates – a routine that usually involved varying degrees of drug-taking. I felt hurt and rejected. As I rather crudely put it to one of my friends: 'I'm alright for fucking but not to be seen on his arm.' We were going out together less and less and, although our sex life remained strong, we were obviously nearing the end. Having caught him out in one blatant lie I was happy to go along with a girlfriend when she suggested our own Saturday night out at my old haunt of the Hammersmith Palais. Earlier in my teens I had been 'Miss Goody Two-shoes' when it came to men and late-night clubs. This time I was in the mood to be naughty.

The guy who chatted to me in the club that night was tall, dark-haired, handsome and well-dressed. As I later learned, he had a 'thing' for designer label clothes, although, then and now, that is the last thing in the world likely to impress me. Having little money myself for most of my childhood, I couldn't understand the appeal of wasting £50 and upwards on a T-shirt. He was about my own age, a little older than my neglectful boyfriend, and things soon got a little out of hand as we danced. After a few more drinks I ended up doing something I'd never done before or since: I had drunken sex with him in a toilet cubicle. It was not the most memorable sex of my life and all I can really remember is people laughing, whooping and hollering encouragement outside the door. It made quite a commotion until suddenly the bouncers cottoned on that something untoward was underway and duly kicked us out of the club. It was not quite a one-night stand; I did see him a few more times but the affair came to a crashing halt one evening when, out of the blue, he decided to bite my bum in bed. It was not a gentle love-bite; this was a full-blown bite on my arse-cheeks that had me yelling in pain. It was the end of a not-so-beautiful friendship.

In the meantime, Tom and I had endured a painful true-confessions evening when he admitted various lies to me and I came clean about my nightclub fling. I hadn't intended to hurt him so much but I am both a terrible liar and terrible at keeping secrets from anyone. It was a little selfish, I know, but if I have a guilty conscience then I always have to ease it by telling the truth. I felt so hard done by because of the way he had refused to take me out but I felt bad because he just looked destroyed from the moment the words left my mouth. Understandably, he said he couldn't be with me anymore and although we tried to struggle on together for a while, it was clearly the end of our relationship. I was sorry to lose him but such childhood romances do have their natural time span and this one's time had come.

There was a bittersweet postscript to my long friendship with Tom. Despite our later problems he had been my first love and the first man to awaken my sexual desires. He had helped shape the fetish and domination interests which have lasted throughout my life. I'd had boyfriends after him, but nobody special and then, more than three years later, I heard he had asked a friend how I was. I couldn't resist giving him a call. The result was a second, six-week-long, fling of 'sex-with-your-ex' which was exciting and fun. With new experiences under my belt I also realised that he was not the best-endowed man in the world and that his cock, which once had been the centre of my world, was distinctly smaller than others I had known. Of course, being the kind lady that I am, I kept that opinion very much to myself and, to be fair to him, the size of his penis didn't stop me wanting to jump all over him again. We had a lot of conversation to catch up on and I felt our renewed friendship was worthwhile and strong. It was not, however to last.

Our second-time around relationship came to an unhappy halt on a Valentine's Day when Tom turned up at my door armed with the requisite chocolates and flowers. As the evening wore on a minor disagreement suddenly turned into a serious row and he announced that he no longer wanted to see me. The shock and my anger made me lose my normal ladylike demeanour: 'What the fuck are you doing?' I demanded. 'You've brought me Valentine flowers, manufactured a row from a tiny problem and then you tell me you don't want to be with me any longer. What the fuck is this about?'

A sudden explanation entered my mind: 'Is this just getting back at me for what fucking happened three years ago? Did I really hurt you that much? Is that what this is?' Despite Tom's persistent denials, I still found it hard to believe that a man could arrive at my door with chocolates and flowers and split up with me immediately afterwards because of the smallest of disagreements. It felt messed-up and wrong and the rejection upset me deeply. We never spoke again.

My first break-up with Tom was to have ramifications far beyond the temporary heartbreak and loss of my first serious boyfriend. For a couple of years my relationship with my grandparents had been easier because of my friendship with a boy they had liked, a boy from what they believed to have been a respectable family. My grandmother in particular had stopped worrying about me being out late or not letting her know where I had been because she assumed that I was in the 'in locus parentis' care of Tom's mother. The irony is that while she believed my moral welfare was being safeguarded by Tom's mum, I was spending entire nights introducing her son to my very own brand of kinky and dominant sex.

Once Tom was off the scene, however, family relationships

spiralled rapidly downhill. Life at home with my grandparents turned into a nightmare for all of us. Many years later, some years before they died, I apologised to them with all my heart for the heartache I had caused them as a teenager. I had never stopped loving them and had always understood that they loved me deeply. They in turn apologised for the sometimes clumsy way they had tried to raise a rebellious granddaughter, both of us recognising that none of us had been trying to hurt the other, it was just a situation tailor-made for confrontation. I like to think that by then we had both come to terms with what had happened in my teenage years. I loved them then and still to this day miss them with all of my heart.

The truth is that I never set out to be naughty but, in my search for teenage independence, I hit the brick wall of a serious generation gap. My grandparents' expectations of what I should and should not be doing were wildly outdated when compared to those of my peers. Speaking now to my birth-mother, long after the deaths both of my grandparents, she admits how poorly equipped they were to handle the situation. I was nothing like an angel, but many of our rows at the time sprang from their complete lack of understanding that teenagers are hard-wired to push against the barriers as they grow older.

My granddad tried to stay out of most of our confrontations but my grandmother and I had a lot of screaming rows, like mega-screaming rows, pretty much always over me not being home. I used to go to school in the week, but then at the weekend I would go out clubbing. And I was working, I had a job in a chemists and I would go out on a Saturday night and then come home on the Sunday. If I said to my grandmother,

'Oh, I am going to be out till late tonight,' she would have one stock reaction: 'Where are you going to be, who are you seeing, where is the phone number? I need to ring them.'

'No, no, no you are not embarrassing me like that... and ringing everybody all the time, Sorry. And no, I'm not telling you where I'll be because I'm not having you turn up there.'

By this time I'd passed my sixteenth birthday but was still being told that I had to obey a 7pm curfew each night. I was a stubborn young woman and the more they tried to be strict, the more they tried to interfere in my life, the more stubborn I became. One constant bone of contention was the privacy I could expect in the house. My grandmother would tell me she did not want me 'out walking the streets', but then would deny my privacy at home. It was impossible to have a private phone call without them overhearing or asking who I was speaking to and if I brought somebody home, she would constantly walk into my room.

'You are so over the top,' I would say. 'Every five minutes I get, do you want a cup of tea? Do you want this or do you want that? If I want a cup of tea I'll come down and get one, or ask you. You're using just use any excuse possible to get into my room and invade my privacy. I'm here, sitting in the house, you know where I am, and you're still on my case.'

Quite often when we had screaming rows they would end with my stomping out of the house and slamming the door, or I would just stay upstairs and stick my music up full blast, just to piss them off. I know it was bad behaviour but it was born from frustration, total frustration. A lot of the time I wasn't even doing anything particularly naughty. Sometimes it would be nothing other than hanging around in the local park with friends but I would still get the third-degree when I got home. I no longer had a boyfriend and although I was seeing guys occasionally, I was always immensely careful not to get pregnant. There were odd occasions, few and far between, when like all teenagers, I would get horribly drunk with friends, but because I had very little money, drinking and drugs didn't figure much in my life. Yet nothing I could say would persuade my grandmother to cut me any slack.

There were times when my birth-mother would try to act as a peacemaker and tell me to behave. I'm sure that my grandmother would plead for her help because after some particularly horrendous argument, Ellen would come on the phone to talk to me. She would frequently lay a guilt trip on me in an effort to change my attitude: 'Your grandparents aren't going to be here forever; you have to try and get along with them. They are doing the best they can, you know, they are a different generation, you have to understand that one day they will be gone and you will feel bad for not getting on with them.' It was all very well her coming the heavy parent over the phone; it might have had more effect had she been there in person.

It's clear to me now that much of the reason why my grandparents tried to be so strict with me was that they had already brought up one daughter, my birth-mother, who had gone off the rails in spectacular fashion by getting pregnant at such a young age. Although they never discussed it with me directly, I think my grandmother in particular must deep down have felt guilty that she had allowed that to happen. The outcome was that they tried to correct what they saw as their earlier mistakes by keeping an even closer control over me. I would constantly say: 'Don't worry, I am not that stupid to have a child, so don't worry about that.' The truth was that I had never planned on having kids, didn't want to get married, wasn't interested in children at all. So I used to throw that at them all of the time. 'I am not the same as your daughter, do not think I am going to have a child, I have no intention of having a child; the last thing on earth I want is to have a child.' They never talked to me about the trauma of the time when their daughter got pregnant. It was a subject that was impossible for us to have ever discussed. I could never raise the issue with them because anything that even hinted about me not being their 'real' daughter was terrifying for them to talk about. It was almost as though an open admission that I did have a birth-mother would somehow take me away from being their child. Because I loved them so much, it was the one thing I could never do to them.

The irony is, my birth-mother was only too happy to talk about it whenever I saw her whilst I was growing up through my teenage years. She would often tell me how she would never have left me with anybody else other than my grandparents... blah, blah, blah... that she knew they would love and care for me... blah, blah, blah. It reached a point where I used to hate seeing her sometimes because I wasn't interested in hearing her story but she clearly had a need to tell me all of the time and bring the subject up on every possible occasion I would be thinking: 'I don't want to know, you don't have to bring it up every time, I am not interested, I don't want to talk about it.'

Partly for that reason, I never built a strong relationship with my birth-mother, and a blazing family row one

Christmas in my early teens led to a long-term break with Eileen – a row that stopped the two of us communicating with each other for years. According to a survey, a typical British family has an average of five domestic rows between the time when the kids wake up to see if Santa has been and the end of the Queen's afternoon address to her nation. Unfortunately, my family was no exception to the rule.

As is often the way with Christmas, the dispute began with the smallest and silliest of 'words' and rapidly escalated from a border skirmish to all-out thermo-nuclear war. After a traditional lunch, with traditional quantities of booze for all the adults, I was playing a light-hearted game of cards with my grandfather and my birth-mother's husband. After losing the fifth hand in a row I foolishly made what was meant to be nothing more than a joke that 'someone is cheating around here. Who's hiding all the cards?' The effect on the winning high-roller, my birth-mother's husband, was startling. He jumped to his feet and started shouting at me. 'How dare you say something like that,' he screamed. As he yelled into my face, I at first tried to say it had been merely a bit of banter but then soon ended up giving him as good a tirade of swear words as I was getting in return. Both of us were becoming more heated by the second but I was still astonished when he suddenly leaned over and pushed me backwards against my chair. I rocked from the unexpected shove but managed to keep my balance and stay on my feet. I may not have been physically hurt but my teenage pride had taken a battering, and my tongue went into overdrive: 'How dare you, how fucking dare you push me like that; who the fuck do you think you are?'

I was in full, admittedly foul-mouthed flow when he suddenly pushed me again, so hard this time that I fell over the chair and went sprawling on the floor. Now incandescent with rage, I was cursing like the proverbial trooper when my birth-mother rushed into the room to see what was causing such chaos and commotion. The remains of the day and our always-strained relationship might still been salvaged if she had just been willing to listen to my side of the story, but that was never an option. She was only interested in the fact that I was swearing at her husband, not that he had knocked me over in a silly row about a game of cards... not interested in what I had to say at all.

Already angry and upset, it was easy for much of my rage to instantly transfer to my birth-mother. 'How fucking dare you.' I thought, 'It's unbelievable. I make a joke and he behaves like that and puts his hands on me, and all she's interested in is the language I'm using.' I was so disappointed in her, so disappointed that she was more interested in the language I was using in retaliation than in the fact that her husband had sent me flying across the room. I no longer remember how the row ended that day, whether I left or they left, but the result was the same either way; I could not help but feel rejected once again by the one woman I might have hoped would stand up by my side. My real mother and I had nothing more to say to each other. Even in retrospect, I find it impossible to judge now how much hidden resentment from the past events of my childhood fed into my feelings that day and over the year or more that followed. Perhaps the row was another nail in the coffin. All I know is that I felt so betrayed that it caused a long-lasting rift.

Two months later a birthday card, containing money in lieu of a present, arrived from my birth-mother. I ripped the card into pieces, left the money untouched in the envelope and sent it back, 'return to sender'.

CHAPTER 13

LEAVING HOME

It was a shocking telephone call for me to overhear. A few half-whispered words that were to destroy the security of the only home I had ever known and leave me homeless, penniless and without a family to depend upon.

My grandmother was in the front hall, speaking with the local social services department and trying to arrange for me to be taken into care. I had never planned to eavesdrop on her; I had just slipped into the house quietly and crept upstairs so as not to disturb my grandparents. Then I heard her one-sided telephone conversation.

'But surely you *have* to take her into care if we can't cope. She's only *just* 16 and anyway what difference does her age make?'

It is hard to describe how I felt when the hammer blow understanding of what my grandmother was discussing struck home. I was horrified and deeply upset, silent tears were running down my cheeks and, in the quietness of my upstairs bedroom, I felt more rejected than ever before. It was, of course, a situation I had provoked through my own behaviour but nothing could take away from the fact that this was the only loving mother I had ever known, now trying to have me removed from her life. I had no real concept of what being 'taken into care' meant other than that it was the sort of thing that happened to girls whose parents had died, or been sent to prison or who had been so bad themselves that they had to be locked up in a council home. The fear of losing the security of my own house, the comfort of my own tiny bedroom, the love of my grandparents and the stigma of council care simply overwhelmed me. Within seconds I regressed from being a feisty, lippy, sometimes foul-mouthed teenager to a little girl who desperately wanted her mummy.

Looking back on that day now, I understand exactly how close to the edge I must have driven my poor grandparents for them to make such a decision. As a teenager, however, full of the fake bravado of youth, desperately trying to learn an adult independence, I could see no explanation at all. As fast as my fears had grown and my tears had flowed, the shock was replaced with an ice-cold anger.

'I heard you, I heard who you were talking to,' I shouted to my astonished grandmother as I flew down the stairs. 'You bitch, you cold-hearted deceitful, hateful fucking bitch.'

Even by the standards of the monumental rows we had on a regular basis, my language was cruel and unfair but driven by a mix of anger and fear. 'How could you do that? If you just

110

want me to go, you only had to ask, not go sneaking off to get me taken away.'

Startled because she had not known I was even in the house, my grandmother did her best to defend herself from an attack which must have arrived out of the blue. 'It's your fault Miranda; you've driven us to this. We just can't cope with you anymore. It's too hard to try and look after you and you don't make anything easy.'

The row was short and sharp and bitter and, not surprising in the circumstances, deteriorated rapidly into my foul-mouthed rant and my grandmother's embarrassed but angry defence. My grandfather must have been in the house but I cannot remember him saying anything at all as I stomped upstairs, banging doors and finally throwing a few clothes into a rucksack. As I tried to pick what things I could pack, I heard my grandmother making another call, this time to my birth-mother trying to explain what was happening. It made no difference to me; if my adoptive mum and dad didn't want me, I certainly wasn't going to take advice from the woman who had given me away. By the time I clumped my way downstairs again there was nothing left for any of us to say. Neither of my grandparents said or did anything to stop me leaving. I was 16; I had no money, few clothes with me, no idea where I might stay and no family left to whom I might turn. As I angrily slammed out of the front door I was, for the first time in my life, truly on my own.

My grandmother had hit an insuperable problem in the telephone call she made attempting to place me in care. Being over 16 meant that the local authority had no responsibility to take me into care or to offer me any support. If she had made the call just a few months earlier, when I was still 15, then she might have had more success. Clearly now, I was going to get no help from officialdom. The truth is that I would not have known how to access any such assistance, even were it there to be offered.

Standing on the pavement outside of the house I had lived in forever, I had not a clue where I could go. Still angry, I wandered the streets for a while then used some of the little money I had to call a girl with whom I had been working in my Saturday job at a local chemist's shop. I have no idea what I told her but, although we hardly knew each other outside of that job, she was kind enough to let me stay on her sofa for a few nights. In fact, I was to stay with her several times in the months to come, although always being careful to find somewhere else to move to at regular intervals so as to give her some respite from my 'temporary' presence in her flat.

Another friend, Julie, also offered me a sofa to sleep on. She lived not far from where my present-day dungeon is located, and unlike my first temporary refuge, she did have the benefit of central heating. After many winters of freezing in my grandparents' home, that was, for me, a luxury beyond measure. The downside of being with Julie, apart from the awkwardness of living on a sofa and out of a suitcase, was that she was in the process of separating from her husband and he clearly resented my presence in her life. I was desperate to find somewhere else to live and then found the answer in being asked out for a drink by a guy who lived rent-free in a London squat. At that time I was mostly definitely not dressing to impress potential boyfriends. The fashion was all for baggy trousers with even baggier tops. But I knew I was a pretty young woman and the guy asking me out was more than passable. He was fit and muscular, a bodybuilder and the sort of guy who did turn me on. He was never going to be a permanent partner in life but moving in with him temporarily would ease my growing accommodation problem and give me a boyfriend of sorts as well. He worked part-time as a bouncer, his squat was rough and ready, on one of the worst council block estates in London, but my choices were strictly limited. I moved in.

To say that my new home was in a rough part of town would be a monumental understatement. Half of the flats were boarded up, no stones had been left unthrown in breaking plenty of windows and it was the type of neighbourhood where even policemen feared to tread. The outside walls of each flat must once have been white but the little peeling paint that remained had long since turned to 50 shades of dingy grey. By early evening, the time when I would arrive there from school, young gang members were hanging out on every corner. I would sometimes watch from my window as the occasional passers-by foolish enough to walk through the estate were subjected to a barrage of catcalls and threats from this weird, drug-addicted boys brigade. Whatever danger my family had feared I was in from going out late-night clubbing was as nothing compared to the dangers I faced once I left the security of their home.

My new friend's flat was on the first floor and so it involved a trudge up a staircase, strewn with litter and reeking of the smell of fresh urine and stale disinfectant which the council would splash around more in hope than expectation of improving the environment. I would often get off of the bus in the nearby high street and walk past those yellow police notices appealing for information about 'an incident' which had occurred a night or two before. There must have been times when they ran out of signboards. Most of the incidents were muggings, or stabbings or gang fights of one kind or another and as I and my boyfriend were just about the only white people living on the entire estate I could not but help feel vulnerable. I was always thinking: 'Oh God, please don't let me get any problems tonight.' We may not be talking New York ghetto here but being barely 16 years old, with no family who wanted to know me, and living in a place like that, really rammed home to me how alone in the world I truly was. Amazingly, despite my constant nervousness, I was never bothered by anyone, a fact I put down to my boyfriend being a body-builder whose sheer muscle-power earned him a grudging respect on the mean streets where we lived.

The other odd thing was that the flat itself, an illegal squat for which nobody paid rent, was actually a clean and decent home. It had central heating, believe it or not, and some carpets, windows and even a working oven. A previous tenant had left the flat partly furnished and my friend had reached an agreement to pay the utility bills so that it still had running water, gas and electricity. It was almost like having a two-bedroomed flat, on split levels, with an upstairs and a downstairs.

On one of my first nights alone in the flat my attempts to do English Literature homework were interrupted by a commotion outside. I saw scores of uniformed policemen sneaking along the wall and then converging in a rush on the building below. They rammed open the door and soon afterwards dragged out a group of guys with all of the accompanying chaos and noise that you could possibly imagine. I was thinking, 'Oh bloody hell, nobody even knows where I am at the moment; anything could happen, somebody could break the door in and I'm here on my own.' I felt entirely alone and vulnerable. When the guy I was staying with got home I breathlessly told him the news. 'Big deal, what's the problem? It's a crack house down there. They raid it all the time. One opens up on the estate, they raid it, shut it down and another opens up across the way.' It was a sobering thought; this was not the place for homework and I had to live here and get to and from my school each day. Life was going to be challenging.

My nights with the bodybuilder had already turned into a sexual relationship although it was clear we were never going to be a dedicated couple. In many ways it was a shag of convenience for both of us. I was 16 and legal now, although he was at least twice my age. Even so he had a great body, a bodybuilder's muscles in places where many men don't even *have* muscles, and was certainly a lot better endowed that the earlier teenage love of my life. He also had a car, so could sometimes save me a three-bus journey by dropping me at school in the mornings or picking me up after classes. He had no problem with me staying with him but also made it clear he did not want me living there full-time. He already had a 'steady' girlfriend who used to turn up occasionally and other women as well. I never minded because I was not looking for romance; this was just a place to stay and I never minded making myself scarce when he had other company for the night.

The downside was that I could never unpack my small bag of clothing and the few bits and pieces that comprised my entire worldly possessions. I would never know who might be in the squat on the three or four nights a week when I couldn't stay. As a consequence I lived a nomadic life out of the rucksack, moving between school, work, the squat, the flat where my friend from the chemist lived and the occasional night on other friends' sofas. The biggest difficulty of all was getting the money on which to live. I had mostly free accommodation but I still needed to feed myself, buy some clothing, pay for my bus fares and just have some money for day-to-day survival.

Work was nothing new to me. I had always had a job of some sort to supplement the tiny amount of pocket money which was all that my grandparents could afford to give me. I'd done a paper round, worked in shops, in a bakery and lots of other things. They were all such crap jobs, and the one thing I did know was that I wanted more out of life than that. I used to look at the people I was working with in some boring shop job and think to myself, 'This is their whole life. How terrible it must be to have no education and be stuck in a job like this, not just for a Saturday or one evening a week, but for your whole life.' I knew that wasn't going to happen to me. The irony was that the only way that I could now support myself and stay at school was to take more of those same crap jobs from which I was so desperate to escape.

So I got a job cleaning offices in the morning before school, and another job cleaning houses at the end of each school day. Then at weekends I managed to get work in a local chemist shop which was close enough for me to cycle to on Saturdays and on a couple of afternoons after school. Between classroom and work there wasn't time for any sort of social life and the only light on my horizon was that I was finally earning enough from my multiple jobs routine to be able to afford a room of my own. I said goodbye to the squat and moved into a tiny bedroom in a shared, terraced house in West London. I still drive past the house most days now on my way to work at my far more spacious dungeons nearby. One of my abiding memories of living there is that I didn't have the faintest idea of how to cook anything. It wasn't only a lack of money which forced me into eating little more than plain rice and vegetables. I was scared of poisoning myself because I had no idea of how to tell if meat of any sort was properly cooked or not.

To meet the rent payments I added yet another job, working as a gardener during the long summer school holidays. A small gardening company employed me to water the flowers and mow lawns for well-off residents in grander, detached houses in a somewhat posher nearby neighbourhood. I often mowed the lawn in my bikini, which may have helped my employment prospects, although the company owner was a perfect gentleman who never took advantage of my admittedly skimpy work attire.

The one thing he did take advantage of, however, was my fledgling business skills and my ability to type. I had done business studies and sociology at school and my boss was studying part-time for an MSc which meant he was grateful for help in typing out his essays. He paid me extra to type for him but then gradually began accepting my input on various aspects of his studies that related to my own schoolwork. It caused some jealousy with some of the other employees because he would sometimes leave them doing the hard-labour gardening work while I worked with him on whatever essay he was preparing that week. I couldn't really understand their resentment; they knew I was surviving hand-to-mouth on my own and yet they still begrudged me trying to better myself and earn a little more cash in my hand.

It was an attitude I had never come across before but, oddly-enough, one I was soon to encounter from a radically different source. The trained and highly-paid pharmacist in the chemist shop where I worked part-time seemed to delight in belittling my own ambitions to get to university. By my standards, he was seriously wealthy, with a large home in a posh London suburb and children attending a fee-paying public school. He obviously thought of me as nothing but a 'shop-girl' and openly laughed when I said I was studying to get to uni. 'You haven't got the qualifications,' he teased. 'You'll never get to university, so why are you looking through all of these books. You may as well accept your lot in life and stop dreaming.' When I tried to tell him I had eight GCSEs and was studying for four A-levels, he brushed me aside. 'Look to what you can get and be happy with that,' he advised.

We clashed on a lot of things, not least the fact that he was so mean he tried to charge me for using too many tissues from a box when I arrived at work with a heavy cold. He paid me just £2.25 an hour but would want to deduct wages if I turned up even a few moments late. Now I was determined to speak up for myself.

'Listen,' I told him angrily. 'If it's anyone that's going to amount to anything, it's going to be *me* – not your kids. They've got everything on a plate, the background and the education because they get it all from you; they've never had to fight or work hard or anything. My parents don't have a penny – but I'll tell you now, one day I'm going to walk back into your shop and show you my certificates.'

It was, of course, the sort of empty threat we all make in anger but years later, I did find myself walking past the same shop and was sorely tempted to run back home, grab my degree papers, stick them under his nose and say: 'See? Fuck you. You were wrong.'

Despite our arguments, my boss's dismissive comments probably helped by spurring me on to even greater efforts to cope with my over-busy life. I also believe that he did slowly develop a grudging respect for me. One day, not long before I left for good, he admitted he had considered firing me for speaking out about his kids.

'The truth is, I fucking can't stand you because you give me mouth,' he said. 'But I can't fault your work; you're honest and you're a hard worker and that's the only reason I didn't sack you then, and wouldn't sack you now.'

The necessity to work hard at both school and in several jobs meant that I had no time for much fun – or for boys. I had become virtually celibate, which was an odd thing because whenever I did have a boyfriend it had been me that had taken the lead in the bedroom. In the right circumstances I was the one who made the advances, hunted men down and generally ended up getting the guy on his back; one friend laughingly described me once as 'a lust-bucket; a bubbling bucket of lust.' Now I was living like a nun.

119

Perhaps surprisingly for someone who has worked for the past two decades in the adult industry, there are a number of relatively common sexual games that I have never got round to playing. In some cases it is simply because the activity does not appeal to me; in others, life has just never taken me in that particular direction. So I have never been to a 'swingers' party, never partner-swapped, never had a bisexual relationship, never really been to any amateur 'orgy'. And my only attempt, so far, at a 'threesome' proved to be something on an unmitigated disaster. When I use the word threesome, I should stress that I am talking of a male, male, female variety – a man sandwich – rather than most men's fantasy of two women with one guy. Not being at all bisexual, although happy to play that part for professional purposes, the idea of another woman and I competing over a man holds no appeal whatsoever.

My threesome 'fail' came not long after a new man moved into the upstairs room above my flat. I wasn't involved in any sort of romantic relationship at the time and was too tired to have any interest in finding one, but my new neighbour, Simon, seemed pleasant enough. Living in the same small house, we slowly got to know each other a little better. He was really into smoking weed, as cannabis was known then, and we shared a little one night. I can't quite remember exactly how that transformed into us sleeping together but it seems to have been our only mutual interest. We both knew, however, that our friendship was never going to be the love-match of our lives; it was never going to get serious. Not long afterwards though, Simon moved in with me, mainly because he was always finding it hard to pay the rent and by moving into my bed he could give up his room upstairs and cut his living expenses. The downside was that we couldn't let the landlord know of our new, shared sleeping arrangements. Simon virtually gave up using the front entrance and it became a common sight to see him hopping in and out of my ground floor bedroom window at all hours of the day or night.

We were only together for a couple of months and, truth was, Simon was clearly a bit of an oddball from the start. On one occasion he took me to meet his mother who lived on a council estate nearby and I was surprised to find that she was smoking puff as well during the whole time we were there. I also knew that he was always poking around in my things when I was out at work. I had a small desk in the corner and things on the shelves would have been moved slightly, or he would ask me questions about people whom I knew he could never have met and could only ever have known about from pictures he must have seen by flicking through the photos albums that I kept in a box in my wardrobe. So, there were some odd signs there but when I confronted him about it he told me I was being paranoid.

He loved to talk about my sex life and ask me about everything I had done in the past and any games that I might like to try in the future. I suppose we were both just putting out feelers to see how this new relationship might work. He said he was interested in getting into my head and discovering what, sexually, would work for me. One night I mentioned that I had never been involved in a threesome but that I might be up for it – if the second guy was interesting enough. Shortly afterwards he brought a friend round to the flat and it was clear exactly what was on both of their minds. Simon and I ended up making love while his friend was still the in the room watching and then the friend moved onto our bed and tried to join in. I was starting to think that this might be fun but then it all went a little pear-shaped. I was up for playing, Simon was still keen but his friend's nerves let him down. It was soon clear that there were never going to be two erections available in my bed that night and that nothing much was ever going to happen. As threesomes go it was all a bit of a failure.

Oddly enough, after encouraging me to have sex with another man, Simon gradually grew more and more jealous and started to accuse me, wrongly, of 'eyeing up' his friends. His obsession culminated in a violent shouting row during which he pushed me across the room. Furious at being physically attacked, I did some shouting of my own and he pushed me again before screaming: 'You want to hit me don't you. Come on then, hit me!' So I did.

My punch to his face hurt my knuckles but also hurt Simon. His teeth pushed into his lip and he started bleeding but it didn't stop him fighting. Throwing himself at me, Simon grabbed hold of my shoulders and then bit my face, just below my right eye. I could not believe what he had done. I think the violence of biting me shocked Simon as well and he just turned and ran from the room. I was left in a state of shock. It was the first time that I had ever been attacked in that way. After cleaning myself up a little I realised that he could return to the flat at any time and that for safety's sake, and to try and prevent him attacking another woman like that, I really ought to tell the police what had happened. The upshot was that I did go to the local police station and reported the assault. They took down all the details, called in a photographer and took pictures of my swollen black eye. The police at that time, however, consistently failed to take much interest in what they saw as 'domestic violence' and so, although they did question him about the assault, no charges were ever laid. They said that the photographs and records would be kept on file in case he ever attacked me again but he never bothered me after that night.

Although I was not really scared of him coming back, I was left in a slight state of shock. For the next week or so I was trying to work with bruises and a highly visible black eye and, although I had my friend Sharon in the building, I had nobody really close that I could talk to.

There are times in life when you need the comfort and reassurance that only your closest family can offer and, for me, that was not an option. Although I had become reconciled with my grandparents after the bitterness surrounding my departure from their house, I knew that I couldn't turn up on their door with my face looking battered and bruised. After moving out of their home I found that I could always pop round for a chat, they would cook me dinner, be happy to see me and even sometimes insist that I stay overnight. I loved them and they loved me; we just could not live together. They were always anxious about me, they were now old and somewhat frail and I didn't want to burden them with my troubles. On top of that, I had at that time completely lost touch with my birth-mother following the angry words that had been spoken during our horrendous row, a situation compounded by not having a phone.

Meantime, although I tried my best to get to school each day it was probably inevitable that with my erratic lifestyle, my studies would suffer. Plain exhaustion and the strain of travelling so far each day was taking its toll. Sometimes I simply didn't have the money to pay for my bus fare, and if I had been staying on the sofa with friends I'd often get woken in the early hours when they came home from all-night clubbing. Soon I was being bombarded with complaints from teachers. In desperation I fixed up a meeting at school to explain that I was no longer living at home and that things were difficult but, with the exception of just one of the teachers, nobody much seemed to care. Still I persevered as best I could, getting to classes whenever possible, completing assignments and handing in essays for all of my subjects: Media Studies, English, English Literature and Geography. It was the pick-and-mix of subjects that I hoped would offer a reasonable chance of fulfilling an ambition to work in television, newspapers or films when I finally graduated from whichever university would accept me.

I knew my teachers were unhappy, but what came next was a devastating blow, right out of the blue. As I stepped up my workload in preparation for taking my A-Level examinations, I was called to a meeting. With no consultation, and seemingly with no right of appeal, I was told that the school would not be entering me for the exams in three of my subjects. My Media Studies teacher was the only one who had stood up for me and insisted that the examination should go ahead; the others had refused exam entry, presumably scared that I would fail and lower their all-important percentage pass-rates and cost them school league table places.

I was overflowing with anger. It was a terrible betrayal, I was working so hard, and they all knew I was, to all intents and purposes, homeless. To make their cowardice worse, nobody had even told me that much of my work had been pointless because they had not entered me for the exams. I was left crying in the classroom where my Media Studies teacher was the only one who tried to comfort me. He was the unsung hero who constantly encouraged me to persevere with my plans for university even though his colleagues had all written me off. The only remaining possibility was for me to pay the fee to enter the examinations without the backing of the school. Living hand-to-mouth on poor wages from multiple part-time jobs meant that it was never going to be a realistic option. Throughout my school life I had always come near to the top of the class. I knew I had the ability to rapidly absorb and regurgitate information in order to sail through earlier examinations with far less preparation than I had completed for these: but nothing I said made any difference and in the end I sat just one of my four intended subjects.

I passed Media Studies with an A but my hopes of becoming the first person within my family to attend a university was fast fading to a distant dream. It was one of my scariest moments: the idea of not completing my education, of being stuck in a dead-end job – everything I had striven so hard to avoid, was in danger of becoming my future after all.

Not, I resolved, if I had anything to do with it.

Finding my way into university at first seemed impossible but I set about contacting every possible college that might accept me. Eventually I found one of the newer universities offering an HND course, with the option of staying on an extra year and earning a full degree. My set of GCSEs and my solitary A-level would be enough to get me in the door, which left only two problems: the need to find somewhere new to live within striking distance of the university campus and finding the money to survive for three more years of study.

I determined to add to my already-tiring quota of jobs to find the cash, but looking for a room to rent when every trip was at the mercy of London bus timetables was proving a serious challenge. I was still in close and loving contact with my grandparents but they had no money and more importantly no car to help me go bedsit hunting.

There was only one other possibility of help: I swallowed my pride and telephoned my birth-mother.

CHAPTER 14

DREAMING SPIRES

Renewing contact with Eileen, my birth-mother, was a huge step for me. We have stayed in contact and remained friends ever since although I will always think of my grandparents as my 'real' mum and dad. It also helped solve my immediate problem as I prepared to enter university.

Eileen drove me around from flat to flat until I found a place I could just about afford, relatively near to my university campus in Watford – hardly Cambridge, the City of Dreaming Spires, but at least it could earn me my much-desired degree. My birth-mother did help me with some rent payments and money for books, but it was still a constant struggle in those first few months finding enough money just to eat and house myself, let alone go out and have some fun. I was holding down several part-time jobs at once, cycling everywhere I could because I didn't have the money for buses, and trying to study as well. I was just so tired all the time that it was hard to concentrate on what I was supposed to be studying. At times I came close to giving up but that would have meant an even worse fate: working full-time in the sort of dead-end job that I was already doing to survive. Every time I even considered jacking the whole thing in, my granddad's word would ring in my ears: 'You've got to get an education Miranda... never give up on your education.' It was his inspiration that kept me going when life seemed impossible.

There was never enough time to do all of the 'normal' things to keep life running smoothly. People think that university students have lazy lives but I was on a media course which meant that even if lectures didn't run till five each evening, I still had to watch films or use the edit suites whenever they were available. There were lots of books or audio and video tapes to buy; so much money to pay out when I didn't have any financial help from my family at that stage, or indeed, at any other stage! When I first moved in I had a cleaning job after studies so would cycle to college in the morning, cycle back to my room, and then between 6 pm and 9 pm every week night I did my cleaning job. On Saturdays I worked in a local River Island clothes store, which left Sunday as my only day off.

About every third weekend I would completely run out of clean clothes. Naturally I didn't have a washing machine and I certainly couldn't afford washing powder and launderettes. The solution was to pile all of my washing into a bag after work on Saturday evening and head for the train station. I hated that half-mile walk and the necessary trudge down the bloody station steps with a passion. The cheapest train ticket would take me to my birth-mother's house in Buckingham-shire where I would load up her washing machine and then often stay the night so that she could drive me back home on the Sunday. She had helped me get a phone so that we could talk once in a while. Our relationship was still strained, there was a lot of distance there and it was awkward but at least we were trying. I was finding it hard to get over my disappointment at how she had treated me the last time we'd met. I was still angry, fucking angry actually, and still felt betrayed and annoyed that she had taken her husband's side in a silly row without thinking of how she was rejecting me.

I really do not know if my hurt feelings had anything to do with the earlier rejections in my life: her giving me up in the first place and then not asking for me back when she had another family whose lives I might have shared. People close to me have suggested that I must have harboured resentment about it, but the truth is I had never known her as a mother, and so growing up with my grandparents was, for me, a perfectly natural thing to have happened. I did have a mum – my grandmother – and so I've never needed another one. On top of that it is not as though my birth-mother ever vanished completely from my life. As a child I was always getting presents from her. She would telephone often and also turn up at the house with clothes or food to help my grandparents' out. She was constantly there as a shadowy, 'big sister' presence in my life – just not as a mummy figure.

My unorthodox lifestyle set me apart from every other uni student. At 19, I was just a little bit older than average but the difference was far greater than that. You hear about all these students having fun, drinking, well that may be the case if you are middle class with wealthy parents. The people like me are the ones who never get to go to the parties because they either get part-time jobs or drop out into dead-end careers with no qualifications. Parties and drinking certainly weren't part of my life because I was working every bloody hour God sent just to try and muddle my way through. All around me were students enjoying their first taste of freedom away from home. They were all 'Wow… I can do anything now, blah, blah, blah…' whilst I was like 'Yeah, yeah, I've been living away from anyone since I was 16. I just want to get this course over and done with.' Everybody seemed interested in going drinking but I just couldn't be arsed because I'd done all my clubbing and drug-taking and partying and drinking years before.

As the months went by I could feel the university workload increasing and time became even more precious. Even bank holidays such as Easter or Christmas were no holidays for me. They were a precious opportunity to get extra work done and earn extra money. I'm trying hard not to sound self-pitying but it truly was a nightmare, a bloody nightmare, to survive sometimes. I had to cycle to the supermarket and buy all these 9p tins of beans and then live on beans and bread and noodles. I had a friend in Southall who told me you could buy these really cheap packets of noodles there, so I would cycle over and pile them up high. I never really got fruit or vegetables, just the simplest things to have some kind of sustenance. By then I was an expert on living cheaply, so I would go shopping with only three or four pounds and come back with surprising amounts of bargain food.

By my second year I knew there was no way on earth that I could do this any longer; something had to give. It was then that a friend, half-jokingly, pointed out an advert in the local paper for 'escort services' in West London. It was a typical massage parlour advertisement of the time but buried in the body of the ad extolling the dubious charms of the 'friendly and sexy girls' was an intriguing footnote. It offered 'good pay' for a receptionist. My friend claimed she wanted to apply but didn't have the nerve to call. I was desperate enough not to care about possible embarrassment; I picked up the phone.

A week later I started my first weekend shift as the receptionist in one of West London's busiest 'working girls' flats. I was certainly not a virgin, I had a keen and continuing interest in fetish fashion and had played what I thought were some pretty kinky games with my boyfriend in the past, but answering the telephone in that flat was an eye-opener for me. Until that moment I had no idea just how many, many men were willing to pay for sex. The phone rang constantly, literally never stopping. Just 18 years old and relatively naïve, I found myself talking to a succession of men about their crudest sexual fantasies. Some of the callers were embarrassed to the point of stammering stupidity, many were clearly a little drunk and some were brazen and just wanted to engage me in sex talk on the phone. My job was to try and make the girls sound as beautiful, as sexually voracious and as alluring as possible without getting the guys so excited that they could take care of their frustration themselves, over the phone, for free. It was a fine line to tread and it also required me to lie through my teeth!

According to my patter, all of the women working there

were 'slim and attractive' all were 'young' and 'eager for sex'. In this telephone fantasy land, the girls 'enjoyed all positions' and were particularly fond of 'the more mature man'. To be fair, many of the women were nice girls just trying to earn a living but this was, in truth, merely a somewhat downmarket suburban brothel, not a high-class, international escort agency: I just had to make it sound like the latter rather than the former. Thus a tubby, 58-year-old prostitute named Irene, with greying, badly-dyed blonde hair and troublesome lower-back pain, transformed into 'Tamsin, a young, in her early thirties, slim sexual athlete with a penchant for swinging from bedroom chandeliers'. I also rapidly became adept at the codeword conversations that indicated the precise services on offer. Many, such as 'hand relief' or 'oral' were self-explanatory, but others seemed to involve a somewhat-stereotyped, racist geographical tour of Europe that took me some while to decipher. 'Does she do Greek?' I would be asked, or 'French without?' Nowadays even well-brought up young ladies would have little trouble in translating those as requests for anal intercourse and fellatio without a condom, but I sometimes got a little lost on this continental journey. With a naturally mischievous streak, I was often tempted to make up my own nonsense terms for a giggle: 'She will do Finnish… and maybe Latvian… but don't you dare ask her for a Romanian kiss.'

Once I got over my initial awkwardness, and better learned the language of brothel-speak, the job suited me down to the ground. Within days I was happily discussing a client's need for 'water-sports' which many of the girls didn't mind, or 'kaviar' (always, for some reason, with that spelling) which none of the girls wanted to touch with a bargepole. I soon became adept at picking out the real weirdoes who just might be dangerous and the timewasters, who just wasted my time talking. The girls were on the whole decent and kind to very young me and it was interesting to hear snippets of the convoluted stories of their lives in between appointments. Most important of all, I suddenly found that I no longer had to worry where my next meal was coming from; for the first time in my life I had good money in my pocket from my receptionist/maid duties. The real oddity was that my own sex life was just about non-existent at the time. I was living like a nun at home but discussing every sexual perversion under the sun each weekend in one of London's busiest brothels.

Throughout my young life I had always striven to gain as much experience and knowledge as I could from every situation in which I had found myself. I started my 'maiding' with the attitude that this was going to be no more than a short-term financial fix to help me survive through to my graduation. Soon, however, I realised the scale of a hidden demand that was not being met; there was real financial potential right here. The mis-match in supply and demand that I had identified was for girls who could dominate men in the way they clearly desired. Answering the phones every day, I would get constant requests for 'domination services' but most of the girls would never entertain that sort of client. The brothel worked on encouraging a rapid turnover of straight sex appointments; the best clients were, to put it bluntly, in the door for a quick suck and a fuck and back out again on the street, minus £60 from their wallets. The girls would charge extra for more fancy games, such as putting on some of the cheap and frankly tatty uniforms hanging up in each room, or for inserting their favourite dildo or vibrator into their pussy, waggling it around for a few minutes and then gasping their way to a patently fake conclusion. For the few extra pounds it was hardly worth their while to bother. They certainly didn't want to get involved in lengthy scenarios with submissive men who wanted to be humiliated or beaten, not least because none of them 'had the faintest idea of how to do that.

For me, however, the prospect was intriguing. I had been fascinated by fetish clothing ever since first encountering Madonna in my early teens. Thigh-high boots, tight-fitting and shiny outfits in rubber or leather had always caught my eye. I knew I would never have the money to buy such clothes for myself; why not indulge that particular passion for my own fun and make money as well. It just seemed a natural progression to willingly stroll down the road to where my own sexual enjoyment could be found. The opportunity to do that came a short while later when a new customer appeared on the doorstep and was ushered into one of the girl's bedroom. There was a brief interlude with the door shut and then the girl re-appeared and told me she didn't want to see this particular client. As far as I could establish, he had asked her for domination services that she didn't feel experienced enough to provide. Seizing the opportunity, I asked if she'd mind if I gave him a go. Moments later it was me walking back into the bedroom while the working girl took a well-earned break. It was a watershed moment for me: I had started the day as a receptionist and maid but was going to end it as a professional dominatrix. All I had to do was fulfil my first-ever client's request:

'Tell me my cock is too small…'

'Now I had graduated... it was time to put "Dominatrix Mistress Miranda" back in her box.' But real life didn't quite work out like that.

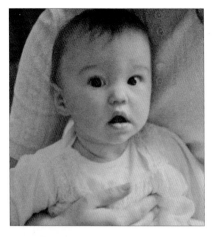 

Above left: 'In the depths of my memory I have the tiniest snippets, like snapshot photographs in my head, of [my birth-mother] being there' – baby Miranda already charming the camera.

Above right: 'Many families have secrets; the skeletons of long-forgotten mistakes or indiscretions lurking in the cupboard for years…' Young Miranda, still innocent of her family history.

Below left: 'But I, of course, did have a mum and a dad, in the shape of my grandparents. They became my whole childish world and my reality: so much so that when Eileen got married shortly afterwards I was recruited as a bridesmaid' – Miranda at her birth-mother's wedding.

Below right: 'I had been a blissfully happy little girl until that afternoon when my loving childhood world fell apart' – Miranda in one of those classic primary-school photographs.

Above: 'When one's parents are in reality one's grandparents there are significant, yet subtle differences that conspire towards presenting a unique experience of childhood.' Miranda with her beloved nan and granddad.

Below left: 'You should hold on to your virginity until you meet someone special, the man you'll marry' – innocence would not last long into Miranda's teenage years.

Below right: 'The truth is that I never set out to be naughty but, in my search for teenage independence, I hit the brick wall of a serious generation gap' – there were still some sunny moments amid the gathering family storm.

'I was a tall girl for my age and even on my limited budget – and even though I say so myself – I looked pretty sexy when I was dressed up for a night on the town.' Miranda before she left home.

CHAPTER 15

A MISTRESS'S FIRST STEPS

The middle-aged man patiently awaiting my attention in the whorehouse bedroom was an unlikely candidate to be into kinky sex. He just appeared to be so 'normal': smartly dressed in a neat grey suit and looking every inch a dull civil servant. He immediately put me in mind of Penfold, the bespectacled, little hamster companion of the cartoon character *Danger Mouse*, a firm television favourite of my youth.

True to character, Penfold was clutching a briefcase from which he proceeded to pull out a stunning collection of items which would never have made it onto kids' TV. He carefully laid out a range of different-sized plastic and rubber dildoes in rows upon the bed. It was, to say the least, surprising, but I was determined not to giggle or react in any way which might shatter my first customer's illusions. The fake cocks ranged in size from a realistic half-a-dozen inches up to a monstrous pink penis so long and fat that he must have bent it double to get into his case. Outwardly I just tried to look stern and commanding. Inside I was thinking: 'Oh My God... what on earth is this lot? What on earth does he want me to do?'

What he did want was for me to criticise the size of his penis and compare it in the most unfavourable terms possible with the dildo cock collection he had prepared on the bed. 'I want you to tell me my cock is too small,' he haltingly explained, his voice mumbling into his boots and sounding as nervous as a kitten. I was, luckily, that day wearing high boots with high heels and so I was already towering over him as he nervously stammered out an explanation of his needs. 'I want you to compare me with these dildoes and tell me that they are what women need, rather than someone small like me. I need you to humiliate me as much as you can.' His demands were desperately light on detail because he could barely speak, either from excitement or fear. Little did he know, but he was probably talking to the only woman in London more nervous than him. My nervousness stemmed from the fact that I had never even considered such a scenario before. I'd always thought that you should big-up, rather than belittle, the size of a man's penis. Outwardly I was oozing confidence but I wasn't feeling confident at all. Could I do this without laughing or losing the plot? Well, I thought: 'Let's give it a whirl.'

I cannot tell you how much fun I had. I started slowly by making him strip naked in the middle of the tiny bedroom with its sole bedside cabinet, a mirror on the wall and a rack of 'sexy' uniforms all chained together. He obeyed instructions and just stood quietly whilst I walked around and around on the tatty grey carpet staring at his genitals. Truth is, I can't remember now, all these years later, whether or not he really *was* any smaller than average. After the first few thousand penises they all seem to merge into one. But I had no trouble in selecting suitable insults. 'You weren't exactly first in the queue when it came to handing out willies, were you?' I sneered. 'How could you possibly think that any woman would be interested in that? You can't even make it hard, can you, it's useless, absolutely fucking totally useless.' As the session continued I was going into more and more graphic detail of how inadequate a man 'Penfold' was. At one point I tried measuring his flaccid cock in inches and estimating how tiny it really was. Then I picked up each dildo in turn form the bed and made him hold them against himself, laughingly pointing out that I was most definitely not comparing like with like here. Spotting that he was wearing a wedding ring, I got more and more personal. 'Does your wife even know if you push it inside her?' I asked. 'She must still be a virgin. You'd never have broken her hymen with that thing. I bet she's probably out right now fucking the milkman, or any man with a decent sized prick.'

I was absolutely loving every minute of the game and, amazing to see, he was clearly growing more and more excited the nastier my creative imagination became. I was being an actress because this was all completely alien to me. I'd never encountered this type of play before. My only personal interest was in fetish wear and bondage play with my boyfriend, and the idea of humiliation was a bit of a revelation because I found it quite exciting and something I could really be good at. Over the years since I've learned that it is the 'feedback loop' which creates my excitement As my client's excitement mounts I get excited by the fact that I've excited him – if you see what I mean. I may not find what I am doing exciting per se, but the effect it has can be a major turn-on. I hadn't thought so far ahead as to consider whether or not he might want to climax but, in the event, he showed no interest in any form of 'relief'. I could have stayed there all day hurling out insults but in the end I thought I had best bring things to a close.

'I can't look at such a pathetic specimen anymore. It's insulting that you could even dare show me something that small. Put it away *now* and get out of my sight.' Then I sat on the bed with my back towards him whilst he stumbled around trying to get dressed. With his clothes back on, he regained a little of the dignity I had so effectively stripped away over the previous half-hour. The transformation was astounding; Penfold the submissive little cartoon creature vanished and a confident businessman emerged. Now it was my turn to be on the back foot as he asked me how much he owed for his session. I didn't have a clue what to charge him. 'I've not actually touched him, just give him all this verbal abuse,' I thought, 'I can't charge him much.' So I just said £30 – the first figure that popped into my head.

Considering the amount of time I had spent in the bedroom and the brothel's normal range of fees, I had cocked-up (pun not intended) completely. Double that price might have been more appropriate. Unsurprisingly Penfold was delighted to settle his bill. 'Thank you Mistress,' he said, 'a wonderful session, thank you so much. You're the best Mistress I've ever seen.' I may have undercharged, I may have been inexperienced, but I'd had a bucket load of fun... and Penfold went away as happy as Larry.

I was happy too. I had just earned what for me was a lot of money with the greatest of ease and without even having to touch my first client. The other girls were impressed when I told them the story, not with the unusual kinkiness of his request but at the way that I had been able to dream up so many insults and keep the abuse flowing. 'How can you do that,' asked one of the women. 'I could tell a man his dick was small, but not in enough ways to keep him paying for an hour.' I wasn't sure myself how I had done it; I had quite liked Penfold but it just came so naturally to humiliate and abuse him and obviously my creative juices must have been in full flow. It was a routine that was to be repeated many times, not always with small-cock insults but with a veritable smorgasbord mix of humiliation that could pour from my lips. I had to use a lot of creative imagination because I had precious little BDSM equipment with which to work. In the weeks to come, one of the other girls even asked to sit in a session and watch me in action. She said she wanted to learn my secrets – but in the end she decided to stick to safer sex.

The fact that none of the other women could handle the domination clients was an ideal opportunity for me. By then I knew what each of them would, or would not do and I knew that none of them would consider performing any sort of anal services on a man. Guys would ask all the time to have fingers stuck in their arses or would want the women to use a strap-on to fuck them. The girls all had a similar reaction: 'I'm not doing that; I'm not touching them there.' So I would constantly be taking phone calls asking for various anal games and I would have to turn them away. I soon recognised that a common theme was developing.

One of the brothels in which I was answering the phones had one very small room that the girls never wanted to use because it didn't have a proper bed. That was not the slightest problem for me because I had no intention of sleeping with anyone and no intention of letting men get close enough to lay me down and touch me. At some time in the past, a half-hearted attempt had been made to kit out this little room as an amateur dungeon. The walls and ceiling were painted matt black and there was an ultra-violet light in the ceiling. A bench sat on the floor and a wooden cross was fixed to the wall. If the working girls didn't ever want to use it then I had to seize the initiative. I was still very much a student and all of this was really just for a bit of fun. But I had studied enough business theory to recognise that there was a market here, with needs that weren't being met. Perhaps I could contribute to a much-needed supply?

I started on a small scale using the unloved room to deal with the submissive guys who called or turned up at the door. I saw some weird and wonderful people but found every one of them interesting and fun. I never tried to judge people and although much of what I was asked to do was way outside my own experience I tried hard to make them happy. There were some things that I wouldn't do, not because I found them too strange, but because they were outside of my own limits. Even so, there were some memorable moments when even I found it hard to understand what pleasure it might bring to a client. One of the weirdest was the man who liked me to stand on his head. At first I didn't quite understand what he wanted me to do but then he lay down on the floor and explained it in detail. He wasn't into boot worship, or a foot fetish, he didn't want bondage or any form of sexual relief. He would come in and I would stand on his head in silence. Ten minutes later he would say, 'Thank you, I'm quite happy, that's fine' before paying my minimum charge for one hour and then leaving.

Not all of the money was earned as easily as that, but soon I was getting enough business to think about buying some equipment of my own to help my fledgling enterprise to grow. I can still remember my first few purchases – in fact I'm pretty sure that some of them are still around my dungeon some-where. I wanted something in rubber, something in leather and something in PVC. The solution was to get a rubber dress, a leather dress and some thigh-high PVC boots. I added a few smaller items such as some lockable wrist-cuffs and a pair of nipple clamps. I planned to use my new equipment in the brothels where I was maiding but also to start offering an entirely new service. I could do 'outcalls', taking my domination services into people's homes. It meant that all of my clothing and equipment needed to fit into one small suitcase (which I also still have!).

This was to be the smallest mobile dungeon in the world.

CHAPTER 16

MY LITTLE CASE OF HORRORS

Looking back now on my time as a visiting dominatrix, I can see that it is one of the most scary things any young woman could do – taking a late-night trip alone to a hotel room, or to somebody's private home, dressed up in sexy lingerie, rubber or leather wear and knowing that your customer is hungry for sexual excitement.

Although I always made it crystal clear that sex with me was *never* a part of the deal, there was the ever-present fear of not knowing precisely what situation I might be walking into. I was tall, fit and athletic and felt confident about looking after myself in most situations, but there was always the danger that more than one man might be waiting for me inside every room I entered. The job was certainly not for the faint-hearted and I soon developed my own regular 'survival routine' designed to keep as safe as possible and yet still allow me to earn my living.

That routine would start with the initial telephone call from somebody wanting to make a booking. By this second year of my life at university I was regularly placing advertisements in local newspapers and most of my clients found me that way. The adverts were very specific and aimed only at men seeking domination services rather than a 'straight' escort girl. Many of the women with whom I have become friends over the years have been escort girls, and I have nothing but respect for the tens of thousands of girls who practice the world's oldest profession as working girl prostitutes. But I have always known that that lifestyle is not for me. By this stage of my life, my own sexual tastes were already clearly determined: I liked fetish wear, I liked dressing up in striking rubber or leather outfits, I liked being in charge, I liked, metaphorically-speaking, being 'the one on top', and dominating men or women was the way that my own sexual appetite could best be satisfied. Working as a prostitute and having to have submissive sex in any way that the man might have desired was the last thing in the world that would have interested me.

For all those reasons my advertisements were designed to appeal only to a particular class of clientele. They would usually say something like DOMINATION SERVICES: UNIFORMS, FETISH-WEAR AND FANTASY or words to that effect and they worked better than I could possibly have imagined. My telephones rang off the hook with guys wanting to book my services because I was the only woman advertising domination work within my area.

I had long known that there were a lot of people who were excited by the thought of BDSM activity but the sheer scale of the demand took me by surprise. I quickly developed a telephone answering routine which, with some modifications, has served me well to this day. The first essential when a client telephones me is to ensure that they are not making the call from a withheld number. I know that many men are nervous about allowing their number to be known in such circumstances, but we are about to enter into a two-way contract here and I need to know with whom I am doing business. The idea that a man might let a dominatrix have his telephone number and then be subject to some form of blackmail or harassment is the wildest form of media-induced paranoia. Quite apart from the fact that I have never wanted to cheat or steal from anyone in my entire life, there is the over-riding fact that I will want you to visit me again, and again, and again in the future. As with any other commercial concern, my success depends on making my customers happy enough that they want to return. I have always prided myself that almost everyone who ever comes to visit me comes back again to repeat the experience.

So, after weeding out those callers who had hidden their numbers, I would ask if my potential client had visited a Mistress before and what services he was seeking. The question can elicit a number of responses: some men stammer, stutter, mumble a few unintelligible words and then hang up. That may mean they were timewasters in the first place, getting their sexual kicks from the thrill of placing such a 'naughty' call and hearing a sexy woman's voice on the telephone. Others may be genuine but so shy about discussing their secret fantasies that their courage fails them. That is OK with me; I am shy myself and know how hard it can be to open up one's secret life to another. In many cases my callers may be taking the first tentative steps towards fulfilling fantasies that have been the unspoken heart of their deepest sexual desires for a lifetime.

Assuming, however, that my caller was still on the line, I would have a brief discussion about the desires they had or would perhaps even prompt them slightly to be honest about whatever fantasy floated their particular boat. It might be rubber, or leather, or the idea of tight bondage and being teased and denied. Some would ask how hard I could cane them, or whether 'watersports' were on offer – never a problem with my ever-ready bladder! The answers from me would always be honest, but always brief. Women in any branch of the adult industry soon become experts in identifying and dismissing the telephone wankers desperate for a cheap thrill and too mean to pay for their pleasures. I enjoy masturbation as much as the next girl but I would rather you performed it as a solo activity, instead of down the telephone line with me. In these internet-days it is easy for me or my reception service to simply ask for such requests to be put in an email; in my younger days I had to rely on telephone skills to reach a verdict about a caller.

Occasionally the initial call would flag up some danger signs. 'There are a couple of us here, me and my friend – can you see us both at the same price?' Such questions automatically earned the reply, 'Sorry, I only do one-to-one calls', and I would keep a note of the phone number. That way, if they called back again I would know not to go there. In those days few people had mobile phones and so I would always call back the landline number to make sure it was correct and then check that the phone code matched the address they had given. Sometimes, despite all my precautions, I would get calls I called 'scrubs', time-wasters who had given a false address or where nobody answered the door. The number of scrubs varied depending on the time of night and you could generally get a feel for them. Sometimes I would think, 'Hmmm I'm not 100 per cent sure', but if I had nothing else going I would take a chance. Sometimes I would get a whole evening of time-wasters, whilst on other evenings everybody would prove to be a genuine call.

Most of the requests were for one-hour visits, although on a quiet night I would accept half-hour sessions: 'whipping and wanking' I used to call them. On the shorter sessions it was difficult to always change into the right outfit. Obviously if the client had requested a specific scenario then I would change but I didn't want to spend my time messing about. By the time I got in and had a quick check around, from the moment I walked in the door that clock was ticking. I would be very, very strict with the time-keeping because I think I charged, when I first started out, £60 for a half hour, £120 for an hour but then it rapidly went up to £150 because that was what everyone else was charging.

Arriving at a private house triggered an automatic safety routine that I followed religiously. If the house had different curtains at different windows then it was likely to be a set of bedsits and therefore potentially more dangerous; if the engine of a car outside was warm, it suggested somebody had just arrived; and if more than one car was warm I would not go in. I would pause by the door and listen; if I heard a conversation I would not go in. My aim was to only enter houses where there was just one guy, hopefully the man who had arranged to meet me.

Once inside I would emulate the guests on the modern-day television series *Come Dine With Me* and insist on having a good look around the entire house. On occasions I have found somebody hiding in another room and have even walked in on young children fast asleep in the nursery while daddy was arranging a bedtime story of his very own. For a while I was paranoid about wardrobes because a man once called me up and teased me that he had watched me in a session with his friend by hiding inside the bedroom cupboard. After that, my checks always included opening wardrobe doors; I never found anybody hiding inside but did uncover hidden cameras trained on the bed. I had no wish to contribute unwittingly to anybody's private collection of adult movies.

The routine was similar for hotel visits, slightly safer because I would always have checked out who was occupying the room, but with the added complication of having to pass hotel security. How one dressed was all-important. I had a selection of wigs because you would not want your appearance to become known to the security staff in the major Heathrow hotels, for instance. Then I would usually be wearing fetish clothes of some kind, covered with a big coat which made mid-summer calls a nightmare. I had one favourite coat for a long time that I bought second-hand in Portobello Road market just because it was great for hiding a multitude of 'sins'. To add to the problem of being inappropriately dressed in hot weather, I would have to wear boots so as not to carry them with me, although I always had a pair of high-heel stilettos as well in my travelling case. Boots or stilettos would fit the bill for most of my clients.

Only once was I chased out by the hotel security – well actually they didn't chase me out, they followed me up to the room. Understandably, the security guys wanted to keep an eye on who was coming in and out of their hotel but luckily my client had mentioned that the staff seemed vigilant and so had given me his real name. As he opened the door I was able to say, 'Hi John, haven't seen you in ages.' And that solved the problem.

The case I would take with me on all of my appointments was a carefully selected little chamber of horrors. The exact contents would vary depending on what the client might have requested and I would have plenty of bits and pieces in the car to select exactly the mix that might please. The most important tools for the job were usually a strap-on dildo, a whip, a crop and some form of fetish outfit. I had something rubber, something leather and something PVC and a couple of specific uniforms such as a policewoman and a teacher's gown. Then came the basics of latex gloves, condoms, tissues and always a bag to put rubbish in. I would squeeze in a few ropes, some leather cuffs, a set of clothes pegs and a set of nipple clamps. Depending on what the client had requested, I might also be equipped with a spare pair of stockings and super-sized knickers in which to dress him up.

With my commercial head on, I would always have a few printed cards as well; you need to do all that you can to encourage repeat business from satisfied customers. As I gained more experience I was always seeking to improve my service and to give the customer more of what they wanted. It meant that I was steadily picking up more stuff; I had to buy a riding crop for example following a customer's request. Then someone else would ask for something different, and so I was always adding new items.

One of the earliest additions to my stock was a set of heavy-duty, professional police-issue handcuffs. It was impossible to escape from them without the key, which one night was to lead to near-disaster. Although I had been playing BDSM games since my schooldays, I was still very much a learner when it came to the intricacies of human bondage. I did not then have the experience to understand the importance of Murphy's Law, that old adage that states: 'If anything *can* go wrong... it *will* go wrong.'

The man with whom I discovered the terrible truth of Murphy's Law was more than a little tied up at the time. In fact, he was handcuffed naked to the metal bedpost in his own house. By this time I had gained a number of regular customers who appeared to appreciate my genuine enthusiasm for bullying, beating, humiliating or teasing them into submission. Among these was Brian. In his mid-thirties, tall and slim with attractive dark curly hair, he was, in truth, not bad-looking and in other circumstances he might have caught my eye for more non-professional reasons. I was with him that night, however, on a strictly commercial basis and neither of us had any interest in an extra-marital affair. He simply needed regular visits from me to make his sexual life complete because his wife, whom he clearly adored, did not share his passion for bondage and humiliation.

Brian had developed a regular routine. Once every few

Shades of domination: Miranda's submissive men behave precisely as she tells them they should.

Above left: One of the classic images of the dominatrix, complete with riding crop.

Above right: 'The beautiful and oh-so-compliant Miss Sherry. She's naughty, feisty, unruly and badly behaved. I frequently have to punish her for cheekiness and for teasing my male slaves as soon as my back is turned' – Miranda's slavegirl Sherry.

Below: 'A filming day is a fun mix of sex, naughtiness, laughter, a lot of stress and what I like to believe is organised chaos' – anything goes in front of Miranda's cameras.

Above left: The type of dungeon room in which Miranda can bring excitement, mystery and, sometimes, fear to her clients.

Above right: Miranda in her riding outfit: 'Once… I have seen [a man] wriggle in pain at the stroke of my riding crop… there is little he won't share with me.'

Middle: 'Your treatment may require a visit to my medical chambers…'

Below left: '[or] the claustrophobic touch of a leather mask strapped tightly across the face.'

Below right: 'Whatever your torment of choice, your role is now simplicity itself: you will obey instantly my every command and suffer or be pleasured precisely as I, and I alone, may wish.'

Left: Miranda dresses the part to attend a bondage convention in Germany.

Below: Miranda and 'the city that never sleeps'. Even an English dominatrix in costume fails to shake Times Square, New York, at dawn in the autumn of 2013.

months, presumably for some family reason which he never revealed to me, his wife would go out for the evening. She never returned before 11pm at the earliest. On those evenings he would book me for a two-hour session at his home. We had a strict timetable to which we always adhered. I would arrive no later than 7pm, we would spend a bare minimum of time on greeting each other and he would then demand to be tied-up and humiliated in every way that I could imagine. At 9pm on the dot I would depart. Although I never saw the after-math, I always presumed that Brian then spent the next two hours making beds and cleaning rooms to ensure than no trace of my presence was ever left behind to alert his wife to my temporary presence in their home.

The arrangement had worked perfectly smoothly on several occasions before the fateful night of my birthday-eve. I had arrived dressed smartly but not overtly sexily. As usual I was freshly showered and scrupulously clean but without any trace of perfume or body lotion that might linger and cause my client subsequent marital problems. By contrast, Brian met me at the door stark naked. His bursting erection was a clear signal of his eagerness to get on with the job in hand. In my youthful enthusiasm to constantly improve my domination skills, I was also keen to head for the bedroom. I had purchased a new bondage toy that week and was eager to show it off. On previous visits I had tied Brian's arms to the bedhead and then, as a climax to the evening's events, I had released his right arm so that he might masturbate himself to orgasm whilst I continued to provide the humiliation he desired. That transition from helpless bondage to one-handed freedom, although necessary for him to gain the release he craved, had always proved awkward. The need to fumble and untie the knots holding just *one* of his hands, whilst leaving the other firmly bound, could not help but spoil the mood which I had worked hard to create. Now I had found the answer: a set of metal handcuffs. These were not mere Anne Summers sex shop toys, but police-issue, inescapable, hardened-metal cuffs that could be opened only with their key.

It was but the work of a moment to handcuff Brian's left wrist to the railings of the bedhead, calming his moment of panic by teasingly dangling the key in front of his eyes and then dropping it safely down into my cleavage. The inside of my bra, and the depths of my knickers, were two havens which all of my clients knew they would never be able to reach. Once he was secured, I set about my evening's task of humiliating him in every way I could. For starters, that usually involved me heaping verbal abuse on his head, telling him how pathetic he looked in the nude, how perverted he was – and how inadequate was his penis.

To divert from my story for a moment, I should point out that a truly astonishing number of men want me to tell them their penis is too small to satisfy a woman. I understand, of course, that penis size strikes at the very heart of their male sense of worth and that it is therefore an easy target, so to speak, for anyone who wishes to enjoy feelings of humiliation and degradation. Even so, I have struggled over the years to understand why even perfectly adequately endowed men seem happy and excited to be shamed in this way. My only answer is that the very act of openly criticising the size of a cock may remove the pressure on said cock to perform. If my teasing words can release a client from any need to compete with every other cock in the world then he may as well lay back and enjoy whatever sensations are being inflicted upon him.

Just for the record, the latest scientific research suggests that the mean length of an erect member is about 5.88 inches (14.9 centimetres) That is a little less than was once thought, a correction required because early studies has asked men to measure themselves – about as unreliable a method as you could possibly devise. My own experience of many, many tens of thousands of penises over decades of intimate research suggests that such a measurement may still be a tad on the generous size. Many men are in reality somewhat smaller than the theoretical research suggests. It just goes to show that you can prove anything with the proverbial lies, damned lies or statistics but I should perhaps mention that I have a slightly vested interest in the matter. My own preference is for a partner as well-endowed as possible, preferably a substantial penis attached to a muscular, body-builder's physique. In the still of the night, however, few men of any size can measure up to the lure of my Hitachi Magic Wand vibrator (or, as the say on television, 'other vibrator brands are available').

However, putting penises to one side for the moment and returning to the thread of my handcuffs story, I was having fun insulting Brian with the sharp end of my tongue, mixing all the verbal abuse I could muster with a few accompanying slaps to his most sensitive regions plus a fair bit of saliva for good measure. Brian enjoyed me spitting all over his body and had a particular taste for being told to open his mouth whilst I spat forcibly between his lips. He didn't mind if it was my natural saliva or if I took drinks of water to wet my whistle before spraying his face and body, anything suitably wet and perverted would do. I had already moved onto some other humiliating games when I realised that a change of position was needed.

From my earliest days as a fledgling dominatrix, I was well aware that the human body was never designed to be strapped in any one position for long. The dangers of cramp, of restricting blood supply and even, in extreme cases, of thrombosis are all too real. I have always made it a strict rule to regularly demand a change of position to avoid any interruptions to my games. In this case that meant that retrieving the key from my underwear in the most teasing way possible and then unlocking the handcuffs still securing his left arm to the headrail. I am sure you are already ahead of me in knowing what happened next. I should say in advance that I am never one for swearing where it can possibly be avoided – but sometimes, as in the opening scenes of *Four Weddings and a Funeral*, only oft-repeated swear words will do.

'Oh, fucking hell, the key's snapped,' I cried.

'Oh, fucking hell, it's what!?' he responded.

'The fucking key, it's broken off in the fucking lock. I can't get the fucking cuffs unlocked.'

'What do you mean, it's fucking broken? Let me out for Christ's sake!'

'I'm fucking trying, but I don't know what to do.'

I will leave the rest of this increasingly offensive conversation to your own imagination. I honestly cannot quite remember the next five minutes in any detail as the full horror of the situation struck home. I tried grasping the broken stump of the key with my fingernails in a vain attempt to make it turn; Brian tried shouting (a lot) and banging his hand on the bed; I tried calm reasoning to work out a potential solution; Brian tried screaming, shouting and weeping with frustration.

'What in God's name am I going to do?' he pleaded. 'My wife's coming home. How can I possibly explain what I'm doing like this?'

I have to confess that I was somewhat at a loss to offer him any positive answers. My customer was not just naked and handcuffed to the bed, but what I did not want to remind him of at that precise moment was that I had wrapped almost an entire roll of brown packing tape tightly around his testicles. Normally he would have had plenty of time to peel the tape off and dispose of it before his wife returned; now time was a luxury we no longer enjoyed. The pvc packing tape had softened slightly in the heat of his groin and his luxuriant growth of pubic hair appeared to be firmly stuck in the warm adhesive. He was literally 'caught by the short and curlies'.

I tried a gentle tug at the end of the tape.

'Aaargh, what the fuck are you doing? You're pulling my bollocks off.'

'I'm trying to help.'

'Well, don't.'

There was another issue which Brian seemed momentarily too distracted to consider but which was literally staring *me* in the face as he writhed on the bed in front of me. Purely to make him happy and increase his humiliation I had earlier taken a black marker pen and written a few choice endearments across his naked skin. The large handwritten words spelled out some of the obscenities with which he had wanted to be described. I remember he had the word SLUT in perfectly crafted capital letters across his chest, WHORE across his abdomen, TEENY COCK precisely where it had seemed appropriate and – although he didn't know it then – an arrow pointing sharply downwards across his back with the instructions FUCK HERE clearly printed across the top of his bum cheeks. Being the kind Mistress that I am, I had chosen a non-permanent ink and I knew from experience that a painful half-hour with a soapy scrubbing brush would have erased it completely. Unfortunately, that might now be 30 minutes too long.

Amid scenes approaching mad panic, I wondered if there was a hacksaw in the house but Brian was convinced his toolkit did not run to such luxuries. Then, I had a brainwave. The handcuffs had come with a spare key. The problem was, it was at my home, and that was almost a 30 minutes' drive away. My client protested vociferously at the idea of me leaving him alone in the house but there was nothing else to do. As I left the bedroom he was frantically – and one-handedly – attempting to pluck adhesive and hairs from his taped nether regions. He had clearly decided that having his genitalia resembling a partially plucked turkey was going to be the least of his problems.

I drove as fast I could to the flat where I was temporarily staying with a friend in the course of my nomadic existence at the time. Running in, I grabbed the key, jumped back in the car and sped back to Brian's home. Disaster! Whatever I did, the new key could not be inserted into the lock because of the broken stump firmly stuck in the mechanism. I thought, 'This is ridiculous. I am going to *have* to find a hacksaw.' So I had to leave him again to look for a local hardware shop – even though by this time it was getting late. There was a B&Q store near me that shut at nine o'clock and I managed to drive there, buy a hacksaw and drive back yet again.

By this time Brian understandably seemed to have lapsed into a state of shock and deep panic and was pleading, 'Oh my God. My wife... my wife... my wife is going to be home soon. You *have* to help me, please!'

Well at least we now had a hacksaw and so I started sawing away at the metal band around his wrist. But these were police-quality handcuffs, not cheap rubbish (I have always prided myself on buying the best-possible equipment) and I soon had to admit defeat.

'I honestly don't think I can get through this. The only answer is I to get somebody in. I'll call the guy who sometimes drives me to come over and help.'

That idea seemed merely to send him deeper into panic-mode: 'No, no you can't do that!'

'Please, Brian, let me get my driver because I cannot do this one my own. I can cover you with the duvet so he never even sees your face; you will just have your hand exposed, nothing else. I can't cut through this myself.'

But Brian refused to countenance the idea and so I kept on sawing, sawing, sawing, making little headway. Then I concentrated on the smaller links in the chain. My arm was aching and I seemed to have been cutting for hours. Bear in mind that I had arrived about 7pm and by now it was approaching ten o'clock – and his wife due home within the hour. Eventually, even though I could not cut through the wrist band, I did manage to sever the links between the two handcuffs and release him from the bed, leaving him with half a handcuff dangling from one wrist, and the other half still attached to the bedhead.

I exited the house as fast as I could because I knew I might bump into the wife coming home. I later heard from Brian that he had virtually demolished the bedhead to get the other handcuff band removed and had then fled to the sanctuary of his brother's home to cut the bracelet off his wrist, for packing tape removal, obscenity graffiti scrubbing, and to compose himself before returning to domestic bliss.

'All's well that ends well,' I said. 'One day we'll laugh at this.'

Brian did not seem to appreciate the joke.

A long time afterwards, I read in *The Times* that the London fire brigade was dealing with an increasing number of calls to domestic incidents in which people had locked themselves to the bed with handcuffs and then lost the key. The spokesman put this down to the '50 *Shades* effect' and the consequent rise in amateur bondage games. Nothing new under the sun, I thought.

The only person in real danger in the aforementioned unfortunate incident was the client himself. But it did make me realise that working alone was both awkward and potentially highly dangerous if anything went wrong. From that point onwards I started using minicabs for my outcalls. It added greatly to my costs but brought a huge bonus in terms of personal safety. I always carried a walkie-talkie radio and let the client know that I was staying in contact with my driver outside until my checks were complete. Then, assuming I had found nothing untoward, I would check the money, start unpacking my little suitcase of BDSM goodies, and let the driver know how long I would be. Literally two minutes before the hour or half-hour was up he would call and say 'Time' and then, if I did not reply, would knock on the door.

My anally retentive attitude to my safety did succeed in keeping me out of harm's way until, that is, one night when a visit to a charming and harmless client turned into a nightmare, with a carving knife being waved in my face as I desperately tried to get out of the door.

CHAPTER 17

'YOU'RE NOT GOING ANYWHERE...'

The situation could hardly have been worse. It was late at night in a strange house and I was being held hostage by an out-of-control, knife-wielding teenager furiously demanding to know what I was doing in his home.

In the background were a screaming, crying woman and her tearful, shame-faced husband. I was terrified and lost for words and, on the other side of the locked front door, was my driver, pounding with his fists in a vain attempt to come to my rescue. Welcome to the quiet and peaceful working world of the professional travelling dominatrix.

The evening had started so differently. I had taken a call from a client who had seen me before, had always paid me by cheque, and who had never been a moment's trouble. He was a pleasant, middle-aged, softly-spoken Asian guy; a family man, living in a quiet residential road in West London. He wanted an hour-long appointment. He wanted to worship my feet. What on earth could possibly go wrong?

Even though I had met the guy before I still went through the basics of my safety routine, making sure that we were alone in the house, warning my driver how long I would be, and safely tucking the client's cheque into my bag. Then I led him up to a bedroom and ordered him to strip completely before laying down on the floor. I wanted his excitement to build gradually as I walked slowly up and down in my black leather, thigh-high boots. I insisted that he keep his head down on the carpet as I paused, teasingly, with the toe of my boot just inches from his face and summoned up my strictest voice:

'Oh, my boots seem to be dirty. Just touch your lips on the leather gently, they are going to need cleaning. When I tell you, and *not* before, I want you tongue-worshipping and licking every inch of these heels.'

The harsher my voice became, and the more insistent I was that he follow my instructions precisely with no hint of dissent or free will, the more excited my client became. I allowed him to run his tongue slowly across the toe of each boot before lifting my leg slightly and demanding that he take the whole of the high heel deep into his mouth. He loved the humiliation of sucking each heel, particularly when I added to his shame by complaining how dirty my boots had become whilst walking to his home. 'I don't want a *speck* of dirt left on these. Get working... harder. That's pathetic, your tongue is useless. Look, you've even managed to miss a bit.'

164

Although my footwear was now so clean that you could have eaten your dinner off the leather, I continued finding imaginary fault, making him twist and turn on the floor beneath me as I pointed out the awkward areas his tongue could not easily reach. It was important in order to give him the maximum satisfaction for his money that I make him wait a while for his ultimate reward: the touch and the taste of my bare feet.

In due course, I made him sit back on his haunches whilst I slowly unzipped and removed my thigh-high footwear and peeled off my stockings. His excitement was by now obvious and I knew he had earned his reward. Sitting back on the edge of the bed, I presented my feet for his inspection. 'You can smell them from there, can't you? Get *really* close but *no* touching. Now, you can lick them clean. Do *not* forget to clean in between my toes.' Now, I am the first to admit that licking my toes at the end of a long working day may not be to everybody's taste but it certainly worked for my client that night. He finally lost control of himself when I first pushed my whole foot into his mouth, stretching his lips apart just enough to cause a little distress and discomfort. A job well done, another satisfied customer and the chance for a friendly chat as he got dressed again and I slipped my worn stockings into my bag and popped my feet back into my boots. With his passion for feet now fulfilled, my client was happy, smiling, more self-confident and chatting away nineteen to the dozen. I could hardly get a word in edgeways as he talked about work, his family and...

That was the point at which we heard the front door opening downstairs.

A woman's voice called out: 'Harvir, we're home.'

Perhaps not surprisingly, from the tens of thousands of clients I have met over nearly two decades, Harvir's name has stuck in my memory. As I hurried out onto the upstairs landing I found 'Mrs Harvir' (as I have always thought of her since) standing on the stairs looking at me in amazement. Far more worryingly was her strapping teenage son, immediately behind her and already looking angry.

'Stay there, don't move. What are you doing in my house,' the son demanded, not even pausing for an answer before disappearing into the kitchen and returning armed with a kitchen knife the size of a machete. 'Who are you, what are you doing here, where is my father?'

I looked around to see that his father had by now appeared behind me. I was thinking, 'Oh my fucking God…' but trying to keep calm and saying: 'Don't ask me what I'm doing here, ask him.' But my client had tears in his eyes and unsurprisingly had nothing to say for himself. It seemed as though the son's questioning went on for ages but in reality it was just a few repeated demands for an explanation of my presence. I did not want to tell him the truth: that his naked father had just been sucking my toes; I thought it might inflame him further. Yet my refusal to say anything was also making him angry. As I stonewalled his questions I lifted the walkie-talkie to my lips and called for help.

'Who are you talking to? What are you doing? Why are you here? What have you taken?'

'I've not taken anything. Ask him who I am. I'm going now. I'm leaving.'

'You're not going anywhere till you tell me who you are,' the

166

son said threateningly, moving closer still, with the blade clearly showing in his hand.

At that moment there was a thunderous knocking on the door. My driver was earning his fee that night by all but beating the door down in an attempt to reach me. I could hear him shouting: 'Miranda! Miranda! Are you OK?'

I have to admit I was so frightened that the next few moments are something of a blur. My client was mumbling incoherently, his wife was bawling and bawling, the son was screaming at me, and my driver was shouting my name. Then somebody opened the door, the son was distracted, I fled downstairs and pushed past into the garden. My driver and I ran to the car and drove off with furious shouts still ringing out after us. We were safe but I was shaking – and then a horrible thought came over me. The client had paid me by cheque and the chances of that cheque clearing had just diminished substantially. That ordeal may well have all been for nothing.

The next day I had a phone call from a woman who asked to speak to 'Miranda'. I hardly ever admit who I am to a cold caller on the telephone; too many callers just want to try and get a cheap thrill out of playing with themselves while they talk to me. So, I came out with my stock reply: 'I'm her receptionist, how can I help?'

'Oh I don't know if you know this,' she replied, 'but yesterday Miranda came to my house to see my husband.'

'No I don't know anything about that; she would never tell me that sort of detail anyway, I just take her bookings.'

'I've been up all night and I just need to know the truth. Can you please ask if Miranda did anything with my husband?'

'Well obviously I don't know the answer to that,' I said, 'and Miranda's busy but if you call back in an hour I'll try to get hold of her and get an answer for you.'

So I got off the phone and I was thinking, 'Oh my God. What do I do now?'

Then the woman phoned back and I took a guess at what it was she wanted to hear: 'Yes, I've spoken to Miranda and she said that she had literally just arrived.'

'Thank God, that's what my husband said as well.'

'Yeah, Miranda says that nothing happened at all, she had just got there and then you both turned up.'

'Thank you, thank you, he told me that but I didn't believe him.'

A few days later the cheque he had paid me cleared through my bank. A good result all round I felt: I got my fee and, as far as I know, his marriage was saved... and possibly, if he ever got the courage to discuss his desires with his wife, even improved.

The incident did make me think for a while about the morality of the work I was doing; not immediately because I was too busy thinking, 'Oh my God, I hope I don't get stabbed', but later when the danger was passed. I concluded that I wasn't in any position to consider the moral rights and wrongs of the married men who booked me because I just didn't have any knowledge at all about their lives or the state of the relationships. Equally, and for much the same reason, nobody had any right to make a moral judgment about me. I could see nothing wrong with what I was doing and I didn't feel then – and I don't feel now – any guilt whatsoever. I am glad, however, that by pure chance I picked the excuse that his wife had been hoping to hear when she called. I was glad to help dispel her worries. And he had seemed like a nice guy; a decent man who was just unlucky to be caught.

Night-time shenanigans apart, my burgeoning dominatrix career seemed to be going well. The money was keeping the wolf from the door; I was losing my inhibitions, collecting new equipment and getting better at my job all the time.

Suddenly having more money rolling in was a double-edged sword. Working into the early hours of the morning meant that I started to oversleep and miss a few lectures; but on the other hand I was able to buy a small motorbike which made travelling to university vastly easier, until I wrote it off in a silly accident in which, thankfully, nobody except me got hurt. I was still in touch with my grandparents and I was paranoid about them finding out about my new source of sudden wealth. I pretended to them that I'd taken a night job in a taxi office, manning the radio dispatch desk. That one lie served two valuable functions: explaining how I had money and what I was doing at night.

There was at least some grain of truth in my story about the taxi company; I may not have been working for them but one of their drivers was by now working for me. On several occasions I found myself with the same late-night cabbie dropping me at appointments, holding onto my radio and generally ensuring that I was not totally alone when I visited strange men's houses. He earned some generous tips from me and, of course, almost immediately cottoned on to exactly what my business was. It would have been hard for him not to notice, given the unusual equipment case I took with me on my travels. By this stage of my life I had not had anything like a regular lover for years, really from when I had split up with my first love, Tom. I was virtually celibate because I was working all the hours God sends and never had time to meet guys. My life was quite lonely because of the turbulent relationship I'd had with my family for years and I was also distanced from my peers at university. I had a secret life that I couldn't talk about with them and they were generally less mature and a lot less worldly-wise than me.

Meeting someone like my taxi-driver, who I'll call Frank, meant that I could at least talk about my work without being paranoid that my secret would be revealed to the world. He may not have been particularly intelligent or intellectually satisfying for me but it was very convenient. That, I fear, may sound mercenary and opportunistic but it really wasn't like that: I was just very much alone. He started flirting with me and I thought, 'Oh, what the hell... why not?'

I can't quite remember the moment when my driver turned into my lover but it was perhaps inevitable, given the amount of time we spent in the car together and the fact that I didn't have time to meet any 'normal' men, outside of the submissives who were hiring my services. We sort of skipped out the dating stage and went straight in, from casual friendship to long-term relationship – going from driving to shagging without dating. I can't even remember our first kiss, it was that unmemorable, but it was a relationship that was to last for the next six years.

Frank started asking me to go round to his home but I was at first almost as wary of him as I was of my routine clients. I knew that he lived with several other cab drivers and it was one of my golden rules never to find myself alone in a house with more than one man. But by now we were at the kissing and fumbling stage of our relationship and there came a point where I could no longer find excuses not to go home with him. I remember being nervous and thinking: 'Oh God, he's the only one who usually knows when I am alone with a client and now it's *his* house that I will be going to.' In the end I scribbled a hurried note and left it on the kitchen table of the flat that I had just moved into: 'If anything happens to me I've gone to this address...'

Our night together was fine, although sex with him was unadventurous and not really to my taste. The one thing he had going for him was that he had previously worked for a whole cross-section of late-night society, working girls, drug-dealers and all sorts. So I think I started dating him more because of convenience and also because he was tolerant to what I was doing. Although our relationship was rather vanilla, it was handy to stay with him because he had no issue with what I did.

I was now in the second year of university and earning a great deal of money; studying by day and working all kinds of stupid late nights. I would whack my phones on as soon as I got back from college in the evening and answer calls through until about two or three o'clock in the morning. Other students often came into university tired and a little worse the wear from late-night drinking sessions. I didn't drink at all but my early morning lectures were hell because I had been dominating three or four men in appointments most of the night. The upside was that I was making serious money. My rates then were around £60 for the rare half-hour appointments and about £110 for a full hour of me being cruel and sadistic to my customers. Compared with the pittance I got for my previous cleaning jobs it meant that I could earn in an hour what I used to earn in a week. The income was somewhat unreliable and sporadic: some nights I made comparative fortunes whilst on other evenings the phone didn't ring. Even so, in what seemed like no time at all, I managed to save up more than £10,000 in cash.

Having that much money was a crossroads moment in my life. I thought, 'What the hell am I going to do with this? I can either copy what my friends are doing and take a year out of uni to travel the world, or I can buy a house.' Remembering how my grandparents had struggled for money all their lives, the idea of starting out on the first steps of building my own property empire was always going to be the favourite. In the end, I put the money down as a deposit on a flat in London, and carried on both working and studying just as I had done till then. My little flat was right next to a station, which I thought would increase its future rental potential, and it cost me £40,000. I think I put down about £8000 in cash as a deposit and got a mortgage for the rest. I was, to be honest, quite proud of myself. The flat I had moved into was the first home I had ever owned. I was just 21 years old, still a student – and suddenly I was a property owner.

My experience of university was nothing like that of my peers. I was never part of the usual uni social scene. When I had the time to join in, I didn't have the money. When I had the money, I certainly didn't have the time. When final exams came around I got a 2.1 which I was sort of pleased with. I probably could have done better but, to be honest, you know, just like anything, you could have done better.

CHAPTER 18

KINKIER AND KINKIER

I thought I was a tough cookie but there's not much that can prepare a young woman for the kinkier side of life as a dominatrix. From the very first session onwards I was doing things that were so far from anything I had done before that I couldn't help but be shocked. It was not as if I had not heard of all of the things that I was now being asked to do: there is after all not much that one doesn't learn when answering the phone in a London brothel. Yet there is a big difference between hearing about the sort of things that go on and being alone in a room with a complete stranger who is expecting you to do them.

One such moment came very early on for me when a guy asked me to stick my fingers in his rear, and I was thinking: 'Oh, I'm not going to have to do that, am I?' It was one thing inserting a rubber sex toy into someone's bottom but putting my fingers in was 'Oh my God, what am I doing here?' To make things worse, I wasn't 100 per cent sure exactly what I was supposed to do once my fingers were inserted, and that lack of confidence was putting me off as well. The experience felt very much like crossing another boundary and all I can say is that once you have crossed that bridge then it is nothing; you almost wonder what all the fuss was about. It is after all the sort of thing that nurses and doctors have to get used to all of the time.

It was the same 'never done that before' challenge with watersports. The first time that a man asked me to pee on him I realised that urinating on demand can be the hardest thing ever. It should be easy but in those early days it was not easy at all. 'Watersports' seemed to be a particular domination fetish for some Arab men who liked to lie on the floor and play with themselves whilst I stood over them and peed. That can be hard to do while somebody is down on the floor looking up your skirt. There were plenty of times when I felt as though I needed to 'go' but I couldn't get to that point. It was awful; the poor guy would be underneath me, masturbating harder and harder and waiting for the big event but it just wouldn't happen. Then you think: 'I have drunk so much, why can't I let it go?'

I saw a television documentary a while back about a famous Australian brothel. One of the women had a watersports client booked but had the same problem. She was drinking and drinking and drinking and I recognised that feeling at once because I used to try and do that to make myself pee. The answer is, however, that you don't need to over-drink; as long as you have drunk *something* and you give yourself time, then nature will eventually take its course. Part of the problem in the early days when I was taking domination calls in a brothel was that there wasn't always time to allow that to happen. With no appointments system, men used to turn up out of the blue and expect you to be able to pee straightaway. One day I had three clients, one after the other, all of whom wanted watersports. I said 'yes' on the phone without thinking through the consequences. The first guy got splattered, the second one got a little damp and the last one had his belly-button filled and had to be happy with that; the well had run dry.

It didn't take long working in a brothel for me to overcome that inhibition. The weird thing is that even after I had become a professional domme and could pee at will over the men, there were still parts of my body that I was reluctant to show. I am a lot braver in my choices of clothing these days than I would ever have been before. Back then I could stand over somebody and pee on them with no trouble at all, yet wearing a short skirt and having my thighs out on show was a complete no-no.

These days, with a couple of decades of practice behind me, I can pee on demand whenever and wherever I wish. A regular supply of coffee helps but I've long since beaten that psychological barrier that stops the flow flowing. The same cannot be said about the guys who come to visit me. It's usually a complete waste of time to demand that they piss in front of me. One guy recently was insistent that he wanted to try something he'd never tried before and so I came up with what I thought was a particularly creative idea to satisfy his need for novelty. Without going into all the hydraulic detail, it involved a catheter condom, a lot of rubber tubing, an enema nozzle and tipping my medical bench slightly in order that he could piss into his own backside. The engineering arrangements worked fine but the human element let me down. I tried a number of nurses' well-worn tricks, such as leaving a tap running and leaving the room so he could pee in private, but nothing could induce the tiniest drop from his body.

Looking back to my early days as a dominatrix I realise now how young and naïve I was at that time. I had never played any sort of watersports games with a partner and didn't even know that people wanted to do such things. It was the same with the anal play that many men wanted. I was completely in the dark. Obviously I knew that some women enjoyed anal sex but I'd never thought about men that way. It is not something that had ever entered into my consciousness, even though I had been adventurous enough to have experimented with rope bondage and had had these kind of play urges myself in the past. I was nowhere near experienced enough to understand all the options available. More importantly still, there was no internet then which might have opened my eyes a little. In this internet age, when every sex game and perversion known to mankind is freely available to view at the click of a button, people are nowhere near as innocent as I was then. Even so, people hear the kinkier side of some of my activities and do appear to be shocked. 'Oh my God, how can you do things like that?' some might say to my face. Behind the closed doors of their bedroom, however, I reckon it is a very different story.

I can't deny, however, that there was an element of guilt

in those early days because I knew that my grandparents would have been ashamed of me if they had ever known what I did to fund my time at university. Whenever I went back to stay with them or just to see them for an evening I just felt, 'Oh God, if they ever knew. It would disappoint them so much.' I didn't feel then – and don't feel now – that I was ever doing anything wrong but I would have hated to disappoint them and I know my family would have had a big issue with my lifestyle.

By contrast, the woman who owned the brothel in which I was working thought that I was a very enterprising young woman. She ran five separate brothels and after a while I started doing receptionist shifts in each of them at different times. I used to answer the phone and leave my cards advertising my own domination services. She didn't mind because she knew I would use her rooms and then give her a percentage of the fee. In theory it was illegal in those days for two girls to be working in the same 'house', but she never regarded the domination I offered as prostitution and so was happy for me to both answer phones and offer the occasional session as well. As the weeks went by, I gathered quite a following of clients who would call to ask for me by name and ask when I was next going to be on the premises.

It was all very amateurish but it sort of snowballed: what started as a simple daily sum of pennies in my hand started to grow into serious money. I would think, 'Wow! I've got my maid's fee and an extra £30. This is fantastic.' I vividly remember the first day I left the place with £150 in my pocket, I felt like the richest person ever because I was only a student, I had no money, and now I had a maid's fee and I was earning more on top of that. Needless to say, I went shopping. There were all these things I needed, like trainers, and I bought this and I bought that and actually got a taxi back from the shopping centre because I had all these bags. It was my first taste of money – £150. I remember it well.

I discovered that with the receptionist work and the growing number of clients who wanted me to dominate them, making money was easier than I had imagined. But I always knew that working in the brothels was no more than a stepping stone, just a way to pay for life until I could graduate and find a decent nine-to-five career. The truth was that life can be unpleasant and dangerous for any girl in a brothel and the muddled-up status of our laws on prostitution offers little protection to the women who work there. Very early on I had an incident when a guy came in and agreed to pay for a session but then started demanding far more than I was prepared to give to any man. I would never have sex, and that was always made clear from the start, so when this guy started demanding more I told him to leave. He walked out quietly enough but then smashed a house brick through the window; I wasn't hurt but it was a terrifying experience.

Soon after that I had another bad day when a client came in and stole the very first piece of equipment that I had bought with the idea of building up my own domination business. It was a V-string, an artificial rubber vagina that could be strapped around a man to hide his own genitalia and make it look as though he was a woman. A lot of the men who came to see me wanted to cross-dress and be made into a woman and so this bit of kit was a logical extension to the normal wigs and women's dresses that helped me create the illusion they desired. It was a big investment for my fledgling business, several hundred pounds as I recall, and it came with variable-coloured pubic hair to match different men and it allowed them to fantasise that they had a fully-penetrable vagina.

The guy who stole it had come into the room before I realised that he was seriously drunk and that there was no way I was going to session with him. I refused to take his money and told him to leave but he grabbed the V-string and ran before I could stop him. Dealing with guys who had been drinking all day and then decided they wanted a five-minute fling was an occupational hazard in those places. I had a lot of horrible, smelly, rude, drunk, arrogant men come to see me because the brothels advertised in newspapers and were at the bottom end of scale. They offered the lowest common denominator price-wise and so it is no surprise that they attracted the lowest common denominator people-wise.

As well as the sort of drunken, scummy bums who I had to kick out, there were other, more serious, dangers. Being ill one day saved me from a horrendous incident. I had been due to answer calls at one particular brothel but had to call in and tell them I was just too ill to work. That same day two guys forced their way into the building, raped one of the girls, and robbed the maid at knifepoint. It could so easily have been me. At around that same time there was a complete nutter, known as 'domination man' who visited several brothels where girls offered domination services. I can still remember his face to this day because he was on an 'ugly mugs' list that the working girls circulated to try and keep themselves safe. His modus operandi was to book a domination session and then beat the women black and blue when they were alone in the room. He put at least one girl in intensive care before he was finally caught and sentenced to more than 10 years in jail.

So there were a lot of guys that were really not very nice at all, which is a consequence of working in an environment where the doors are open to all. Men call the number in an advert, you give them the address and they turn up at the door. Even though I found that those who sought fetish services tended to be more educated, intelligent and articulate people, it didn't alter the fact that you are not selecting your clients, they are selecting you. It creates a very different clientele to the one I have now.

Back then, and in all the many contacts I've had over the years with 'working girls' – the euphemistic name for prostitutes – I've never come across any woman in the sort of forced-labour situation which seems to have obsessed the police and the popular press in recent years. I don't doubt that there are the very occasional cases where girls are exploited by evil trafficking gangs, but the image that is peddled that this is all part of widespread organised crime is far from the truth. Do I feel there are woman exploited? I can't say that I have ever seen it in any of the brothels I ever knew of, and ever worked in and answered the phones. Those girls were certainly not exploited. Some of course will be taking drugs but that is a very different problem and, again, most of them are not forced into it at all. Many of them are quite happy, like me they quite enjoy what they are doing, not all of it is doom and gloom. Depending on where they work, prostitutes can come into contact with decent, interesting people.

I certainly found most of my clients interesting in the days when I was building up my outcalls domination service throughout the London suburbs. Clothing was an important consideration once my workload increased. I needed clothes that could cover whatever kinky outfit I was wearing underneath and could be versatile enough not to look out of place going into a private home or a London hotel. You wanted to go looking sexy and smart but not so sexy that the neighbours would stare at you, and not so smart that it just looked wrong. I used to wrestle with myself wondering should I wear a business suit, or should I wear normal clothes just to blend in as though I were a friend calling round to the house? It was a constant dilemma and I went through phases of trying out different things. At one stage I thought of putting a uniform on and just brazening it out on the streets but then I thought, 'What if I get stopped by the Old Bill, having a uniform on? It could be disastrous'.

The worst time for outcall appointments was summertime because it was so much harder go dressed up in fetish-wear during the lighter, warmer nights. I tried to wear my boots so that I did not have to carry them with me, but they looked out of place in midsummer.

The other thing I didn't like about summer was that it got dark so late that I would be arriving at places in bright daylight rather than in the dark. Summer nights made me stand out more. I would be heavily made-up and probably carrying a suitcase to the door as though I was moving in for the weekend – a young woman, about 21, wearing a wig. I just stood out. To try and blend in, I used to buy those bustier-type tops where the front would come to a 'V' with wider straps which would uplift you to create a bit of a cleavage. I would select ones in satin, like an electric blue satin with a black satin skirt. It was a little like club-wear but you could just sling a corset and some boots on and it really dressed it up – daywear that looked sexy. It meant it was somewhere between the two and I could wear it in the summer although it looked eye-catching and smart enough to impress a client.

Frank, my minicab driver, had by now moved in with me at my new flat and we settled down to a rather sexless, dull but convenient relationship. He said he loved me but I think, in truth, it was a convenient pairing for him as well. He certainly liked the fact that I was earning a great deal of money. I did have feelings for him and he did have feelings for me but I never considered that it would be a life-long commitment. These days I try to wipe him out of my memory, not least because of the way he betrayed me at the end of our relation-ship. He could be very controlling at times and he did his level best to ensure that I kept my distance from my birth-mother and that generation of my family. 'Don't you realise what she's done to you?' he would say. 'They all rejected you… you should reject them. Why should you have any contact at all?' His dislike of my family was part of his manipulative, yet childish nature. He could be unpredictable, argumentative and insecure all in one; not a very attractive package. When we did have arguments he found a powerful way to threaten me. He knew that I was paranoid about my ageing grandparents finding out about my secret life of kinky sex. So he constantly threatened to tell them.

He didn't have any moral objection to my work and seemed to have little jealousy about me meeting other men. He was certainly only too pleased to be accepting money to drive me around from place to place but then would use threats to try and control me. I think in retrospect I only stayed with Frank for as long as I did because of that often-voiced threat to expose my working life to my much-loved grandparents. He was an arsehole excuse for a man but I truly feared that the shock might kill them so I put up with far more from him than I should have done.

Sadly, it was to end very badly.

CHAPTER 19

A NORMAL JOB

I have never had any concerns about the morality of my work and have never felt that what I do for a living is wrong. In fact, I think I do a lot of good for a lot of people, and no harm whatsoever to anyone.

I am happy that I make people happy, even though the way that I make people happy may not be the norm. The satisfaction that I bring to people's lives is not the norm, but I feel I do have an impact in a positive way on a wide variety of people. I can be an understanding ear listening to my clients' desires in a part of their lives which their own partners or their closest friends might not understand or condone. I can be a reliever of the stress of their everyday lives. One of the nicest parts of my job is being told by men and women that their lives are the richer for having met me.

There did come a time however, after I had been doing

outcall domination for about a year, when I started worrying about the effect my chosen career could have on my family. My grandparents were still alive and I knew they would be devastated were they ever to find out about my work. I felt guilty when I looked at them, thinking to myself, if they knew my life and what I do to pay my way through university, I would be such a disappointment to them; and I would have hated to disappoint them. That was the time when I questioned my chosen path because I looked at them and I thought they are such a different generation, so much older than my parents should logically have been and therefore utterly divorced from my world.

My fears grew after a series of exposé stories in newspapers such as the *News of the World* publicly identified several pro-domme girls operating in London. I also knew that my job was gradually isolating me from friends and family. Nowadays I know, and count as friends, many of the women working as pro-dommes in the UK, along with a good few of my European and American counterparts. In the 1980s there were few other girls in my line of work and the need for secrecy kept us from even attempting to befriend each other. Now, I wanted to have a good stab at trying to do a normal job and have normal friends. The hours were crazy doing outcalls; it is all nights and you end up sleeping all day and just being out of society, isolated and out of a normal life and normal conversation and normal things.

Perhaps more importantly, I had never intended being a dominatrix to be my long-term career path. It was merely a way of making enough money to keep the wolf from the door whilst I studied for three years at university. Now I had graduated, I had my degree (a 2.1, since you kindly ask, or did I mention that already?) and had been thoroughly trained for a future career in the media. I felt my life was full of future promise and was anxious to get started. It was time to put 'Dominatrix Miss Miranda' back in her box and let butter-wouldn't-melt-in-my-mouth Miranda, career girl extraordinaire, out into the limelight. It was time to get a 'proper' job.

My friends know that once I make a decision I can brook no delay in implementing it. So I cancelled my newspaper advertisements, told clients who called that I was no longer in business, and threw away much of my expensive equipment. I was determined to be 'normal', but the truth was, I could not quite bring myself to part with every single one of my toys. In fact, there are one or two items, including a favoured and much-used strap-on dildo and a couple of rubber outfits, which I still keep in my sexual armoury to this day. I was however determined to be normal. I had to be normal – a state I achieved only to find it was a horribly miserable state in which to be.

What I had not counted on in my rush to achieve respectability was that the media, where I chose to forge a new career, is one of the greatest bastions of nepotism left in the country. I soon found out that unless one had a mother or father 'in the business' or unless one was prepared to work for months as an unpaid 'runner', there were precious few ways of breaking into the tightly closed shop of broadcasting or films. By sheer dogged perseverance however, and by toning down my early ambitions to become the Director-General of the

BBC, I did finally manage to land a job. It was with a company which hired out equipment to television and feature film producers. 'It may not be *Panorama*,' I thought, 'but it is at least a foothold in a competitive industry.' I determined to be a dedicated and loyal employee; I knew I had studied hard and was willing to learn more; surely I could work my way upwards in this new chosen career? How wrong could I be.

My job was helping clients book the equipment they might need for any sort of filming activity. Our customers ranged from major film studios through to advertising agencies and commercial broadcasters. People would call seeking 'dollies' or 'tracks' for the cameras and I would ensure they were ordering exactly what they needed. There was little that was creative about my role, but it did at least mean I was using some of the filming knowledge I'd accumulated at university. I was enthusiastic, grateful to have found a toehold in the most competitive of industries and determined to be promoted and progress through the company hierarchy as fast as possible. Even though I say it myself, my ambition made me a first-class employee; I was always on time, was very efficient, very organised. Because I was always the first one into the office each morning I would take the heaviest workload of the day and also answer all of the many incoming calls for the hour or so before the part-time receptionist arrived at work. If I wanted food, I would call up to the canteen and they would bring something down so that I didn't have to break from my desk and the phones.

For the first few months, I enjoyed the work and never complained about the workload. I was well-used to hard graft for long hours, even though this career was, of course, a radical departure from the far more private work I'd been doing until then. Then reality dawned and I gradually realised that whilst myself and a couple of other girls were working like crazy, there was an entire team of male middle-managers who were doing nothing productive at all. On the contrary, they would often ruin the system by double-booking-out equipment for a glamorous project like a new feature film, with no recognition that the company bread-and-butter clients were being shafted at the same time. I used to find it utterly frustrating because I would be doing exactly what I was supposed to do but they would be causing chaos. I also realised that there was little chance of my being promoted because these guys were going nowhere; they were receiving good money and having an easy life whilst we did the work.

Bizarrely, the realisation that I was being exploited pushed me into working even longer hours – but this time for myself rather than exclusively for my employer. I had been working in the media for long enough by then to know that either working for nothing for months of so-called work experience, or using old-fashioned nepotism, were almost the only way of breaking into the industry. With a mortgage to pay and no family to help, I couldn't afford to work for free and it seemed that even lowly researchers had to be related to established executives before they could gain an interview. With my family background, I was the least connected person imaginable. I had to come up with a plan. That was when I started getting into work even earlier and staying even later in order to look through the company's extensive lists of contacts within a myriad of media concerns. Then, working at home in the evenings, I would write to each and every company, often to named individuals from those contact files, looking for a job that might progress my career. Out of the 900 or so letters and CVs which I posted over the next few months I received a number of replies offering an interview. Quite a low number... well... to be precise... just two.

It was heart-breaking receiving rejection after rejection and seeing the 'thank you, but sorry...' letters pile up in my files. Even the couple of interviews I did get were dispiriting. One woman started by announcing: 'Basically, we're looking for a dogsbody.' I still did my best to impress her but, inside, I was thinking, 'I can't believe that's the way you kicked off my interview. You may be looking for your dogsbody, but I want a career.' I knew that my experience was limited but I'd studied hard and I did have a degree, and I'd been interested in working in television for many years. When I was 16, I'd pestered to get work experience in the BBC newsroom, going out with news crews, going into the edit suites and then seeing how the evening news is put together. Talking to the camera-men convinced me that I wanted to be a camera operator – even though people tried to tell me it wasn't a job for a girl. 'It's outside work and you have to lug all the equipment around,' one cameraman told me. 'You'd be better off thinking of something inside the studios that's more suitable for women.' Clearly, I thought at the time, the BBC's anti-sexism training isn't yet up to speed.

My equipment bookings job was paying me around £1000 a month before tax. That was just enough for me to survive on and pay my mortgage, although I knew I could once have earned that much cash in just one night. Even so, despite my growing dissatisfaction, I didn't say anything or complain because I was conscious that this was my very first 'real' job and I truly wanted to succeed. Then, some months later, I learned that one of the guys had been promoted to a junior manager position and that cut me to the quick. We had joined the company at around the same time, I knew he had a lesser degree than me, he was slightly younger than me and, most irritating of all, I knew he spent half of his time at work chatting to people in the warehouse whilst I was doing my job and making them money. I looked at the situation from every which way I could but, as far as I could see, the only thing my rival had going for him was that he was a man. All the managers were men, all the underlings were women. I had heard the phrase 'glass ceiling' before but it was still a shock to bump up against it.

Seeking some sort of recognition for the efforts I had been putting in, I asked for a pay-rise, but the idea was dismissed on the grounds that paying more to me meant they would need to pay more to others – which felt like no sort of a reason to deny me at all. Soon afterwards I handed in my notice. At the leaving interview I made it clear that I felt their company was anything but progressive for the female staff.

Out of a job and with no further offers of interviews, I might have been in trouble. There were a lot of people chasing too few jobs. Unlike many of my contemporaries, however, I did at least have Plan B.

CHAPTER 20

'EVERYTHING GOES UP… APART FROM THE PRICE OF PUSSY'

Starting out in my own business as a professional dominatrix was both the most exciting, and the scariest thing I had ever done. This was my Plan B: to try and revitalise the domination work I'd abandoned when I found gainful 'straight' employment.

Unfortunately, I'd been so determined to leave my previous lifestyle behind me and build a normal career that I'd ditched most of the thousands of pounds worth of BDSM gear I'd collected for my outcalls business while at university. I had deleted the telephone numbers of clients from my phone and anybody who had called me had been told that I had given up my domination work for good. I faced rebuilding what had been a successful and thriving business from scratch but was utterly determined to succeed, one way or the other. If dominating men was how I was going to make my mark and earn a good living, then that's was what I was going to do. I had one big advantage: I now owned a flat which I had originally intended to rent out to supplement the meagre income from my media career. I'd originally bought it with its rental potential very much in mind. Now it was the ideal base for my domination future.

Despite my earlier experience in various brothels and my outcall efforts, I still had little real idea of my clients' needs and requirements. I had been very much self-taught. I know now that most girls in my situation learned their tricks of the trade from older, more experienced Mistresses. All I had to guide me was my own genuine sexual interest in dominating men. However, 'nothing ventured, nothing gained' and so I cobbled together a local newspaper advert for 'Domination Services' and waited to see what would happen. My best guess was that I might get a few freak calls, but that would be about it.

That was when my telephone started ringing off the hook.

From day one, my new domination career was up and running – fast. The phones rang; the men kept coming, and then coming back for more. I may have been inexperienced but I was clearly doing something right. Perhaps, most importantly, I was indulging many of my own interests. I can't deny I got a kick out of my pro-domming and I enjoyed being as creative as I could be. That holds good to this day. To build any kind of BDSM scene you have to enjoy the scene yourself. Having a creative mind to build interesting scenarios, combined with my own interest in the fetish scene, were among the factors which brought me rapid success.

The other reason that the calls kept on coming was that there were at that time so few professional dominatrices working in London. It was very much a niche market with little serious competition. I like to think, though, that my strong work ethic was also a factor. Unfortunately, it is not always shared by all of the other girls who have since entered the profession. Unlike some, I pride myself on always keeping appointments and being available at the times when I have said I will be available; I never cheat people out of the time for which they've paid; and I work hard to give my clients the experience they desire.

In that era, it was also a lot easier to say what I wanted to say in newspaper advertising than it is today. I would use copy lines that would never be accepted by the more prudish newspaper industry now, such as referring to myself as the 'notorious Mistress Miranda' and mentioning sex toys and strap-ons and uniforms. The chance to boast about my wider range of services was important because so many potential clients wanted to go beyond just being spanked or caned. Many people seem to think that domination is all about corporal punishment of various kinds but that is far too simplistic a view. It was important to me to stress that I was not simply offering hard-core beatings, although I was happy to offer a black-and-blue beaten bottom if required. But many of my clients wanted simply to dress in women's clothing or indulge in elaborate role-play. I tried to reflect those choices in all my advertising which brought me a lot of calls. So many that I could hardly answer them all.

My fledgling business did well from the start, which was slightly surprising because I was having to pick up a whole new range of business skills as I went along – very much 'learning on the job' you might say. I worked out my pricing policy, for example, by studying the going rate for general 'incalls' in massage parlours and adding a bit extra to reflect the fact that I was offering an unusual service. One of my friends who ran a brothel would keep me up to date with current rates. 'You should always charge more for the sort of domination services you offer,' she would say. That's why I soon went up to £150 for an hour, a price I maintained for many years. My pricing policy was, however, partly deter-mined by an old saying within the adult industry: 'Everything goes up, apart from the price of pussy.'

It is amazing that the sex business seems to be immune from the general impact of inflation. That means that even 20 years ago, when I was answering telephones in a London brothel, clients were charged £60 for what prostitutes call a 'full personal service'. If you telephone any brothel now, a full two decades later, you will find it is *still* £60 for a full personal service. Other rates will also be much the same now as they were then: £30 for topless hand-relief, £40 for a full strip, and £50 for oral sex. I think that what has happened is that decades ago the shame accompanying prostitution meant that few girls dared to move into the game: now that society's attitude has changed, more and more girls are willing to trade on their feminine assets for cash. That vastly increased supply has kept prices down.

Hence, 'everything goes up apart from the price of pussy'.

Self-conducted market research helped me decide which services I should offer to attract more clients. I scoured other adverts in newspapers and on advertising cards to see what domination delights my competitors were offering. I would look at them to check out what they were offering that I wasn't. Then, whatever it was, I wanted it – I wanted to be able to do it. I noticed, for instance, that one woman mentioned 'electrics' and I thought I ought to do the same. The problem was that I didn't have the faintest clue what 'electrics' might involve. I feared that plugging my clients into the mains supply might soon reduce my customer base, but what else could she mean? I soon discovered that she was using a form of electric exerciser that delivered a safe level of current through pads or wires to different parts of the body. A client's nipples, arse, cock and balls are all favoured locations for a short, sharp zap of electricity. The sensation is much like the static electric shocks that we all suffer once in a while in everyday life. The difference is that these shocks hit you over and over and over again and there's nothing you can do to stop it. It sounded like fun! I duly researched the possibilities until I found something similar, saved up to buy as much of the equipment as I could possibly afford and practised until I was perfect.

Nowadays I pride myself on having the most comprehensive range possible of electrics boxes and the plugs, pads, clips and leads to deliver a little – or a lot – of pain. Many of my clients love to suffer the treatment, and the act of having an electric 'butt-plug' roped into place is often the first stage of their complete submission to my will in any session. It's humiliating and uncomfortable to have their anal sphincter penetrated – it makes them slightly fearful of the discomfort and pain I can induce at the touch of a button –

and once their interfering hands are tied out of the way, it puts them completely at my mercy. All in all, the perfect start to a consultation with me.

My acquisition of the electrics boxes (I now keep at least half a dozen of them around the dungeon at any one time) perfectly illustrates one of my business strengths – and weaknesses – all in one go. I love gadgets and have to have everything new as soon as I see it. It's a character trait that probably goes right back to my teenage years. Thinking back to when I was about 16, I would see pictures of icons such as Madonna in PVC or leather fetish clothing and think, 'Oooh, I want to look like that.' Unlike some other teenage girls I didn't see pictures of white wedding dresses and wish it was me. I saw black corsets and thought, 'That is what I want to look like.' Even if I was not a pro-domme Mistress I would still want to dress in that way. For me, this has never been a job, it's a vocation. But such acquisitiveness is a double-edged sword for my business: it puts up my costs a lot but also means that my clients can expect something fresh and different with every visit.

In my early days, with a limited income from a limited number of clients, I had to make do with whatever equipment I could get. I was such a novice that I didn't even know where I might buy the type of specialist equipment that nowadays graces all of my rooms. So my bondage equipment was very basic and a lot of it was homemade. My partner knocked a few things together out of some wood, including a bondage bench by the simple expedient of screwing some leather straps onto a fold-up, portable massage table. Unfortunately both his DIY skills and the lightweight table were rubbish. I had one client who was quite big, and in mid-session the table collapsed: hugely embarrassing, as you can imagine. It didn't collapse completely but just cracked under his weight. Luckily he wasn't hurt, but he was mortifyingly embarrassed. 'I am so sorry I have broken your table. I am really sorry,' he kept saying. I felt bad for him and tried to reassure him that I wasn't angry and it hadn't been his fault, but he wouldn't stop apologising and was still distraught when he left. For ages afterwards I was certain that I had lost him as a client but then he turned up again out of the blue. The transformation was amazing. He told me he had lost four or five stone in weight from exercising and eating more healthily after the massage table disaster. It was a powerful recommendation for the 'Miss Miranda diet plan', if not for the quality of my equipment.

That incident prompted me to take a new look at my business philosophy. I thought: 'This is ridiculous. I have to have stronger stuff, better equipment.' Perhaps I shouldn't be trying to make do and mend. Perhaps I needed to have faith in myself and invest properly in the future. I realised that any business needs to constantly invest in itself to succeed. It's a philosophy that I have followed to this day and have never regretted. The consequence was that my next purchase was a high-quality, metal-framed, revolving bondage rack that cost me far more than I could really afford at the time. I needed it to be strong enough to cope with the heaviest clients, and be free-standing so that I could take it with me if I ever moved premises. It has been with me ever since and now, almost two decades later, still stands in the suspension room of my London dungeon, even though it is the piece of equipment I probably use least of all. The reason for that is that I have learned from experience that you need to be careful of locking clients into an upright position. I have never harmed any of my clients but I have learned of the very real danger they might faint.

Men and women do faint in my chambers from time to time and I am always meticulously careful to ensure that any bondage positions I use will keep them safe and secure if that happens. Even before they arrive at the dungeon they may have taken tablets such as Viagra which can lower their blood pressure, or 'poppers', tiny inhaled doses of amyl nitrate which have a similar effect. Nobody should ever consume a combination of the two but I have no control over what they may have used before they walk through my door. More frequently, my clients may wish to be wrapped in multiple rubber or leather layers that can make them hot, even within my air-conditioned rooms. Add in the fact that they're excited and nervous and want tight straps across their chest and it's not surprising that people can easily faint. They all almost always say 'I've never fainted before', but it take just a second for your body to decide that it wants to shut down and lay flat to recover. Everyone comes round again mega-fast but they do have a range of reactions. Some feel just a little bit woozy, while others yell as though you have tried to kill them or something. It's just the panic of being out of control. It is also the reason why I rarely use bondage with clients standing up.

I learned that lesson in my early days when a large man suddenly fainted whilst standing upright on my revolving bondage rack. He was strapped in securely and going nowhere, but the way in which he slumped down meant that a strap was forced up underneath his chin. I was thinking, 'Oh

202

my God, how am I going to get him undone.' The guy was out cold, a total deadweight, and it was taking all my strength to try and lift him. Then I realised that I also had his feet tied to the rack. I somehow had to hold him up and release those ankle straps as well. It was terrifying but somehow I found the strength to keep the pressure off his neck and release safely. He wasn't hurt and came round immediately without ever knowing what had happened. But I vowed never to go through that experience again. Now my clients' safety is always at the forefront of my mind. I may be paid to hurt or humiliate them – but the truth is that, with the rarest of exceptions, I enjoy their company and like them all.

Many of my clients enjoy the texture of rubber but one of my first customers had a stronger obsession than most. 'Rubber Ian', as he called himself, was a married man with an obsessive rubber fetish to rival any I have ever seen. He was memorable because he was the only rubber client I had ever had who took his fantasies home and played them out in front of his long-suffering spouse. His wife thought he was barmy because he would put on rubber outfits and traipse around their home in rubber boots, rubber suit and rubber gas mask. He would just sit at the breakfast table in his rubber gear, or put a hood on, watch TV, or do his crossword. What I found fascinating was that his wife would leave him to it. She did not know that he visited me, but she knew that he went to 'professional ladies' to dress in his beloved latex. And that was all he did: dress up himself and ask them to dress in rubber as well. He would always bring items for me to wear in our sessions and it gave him a thrill to see women in rubber while he was dressed in a similar way. He didn't seek any sexual contact. He wasn't a young man and, although he used to touch himself through all his layers of rubber, he never relied on me to give him any form of relief.

I still have some of the rubber hoods and a cape that he gave me all those years ago. He was such a regular client but then one day he just stopped calling and I never heard of him again. It is one of the oddities of my profession that people can become influential in guiding me towards a better understanding of a particular fetish desire, and then suddenly vanish from my life. I wondered for some time if he had died or just moved away: I never have much knowledge of clients' 'normal' lives outside of my dungeon.

There is a popular but totally inaccurate image of the type of men who visit a dungeon. Some people might look down on them because of their sexual tastes, but I would never do that; how could I when I share most of those tastes myself? They are pictured as 'dirty old men in raincoats' but the reality could not be more different. Most of my clients are educated, intellectual and in positions of power and responsibility. The truth is that they have to be as successful in order to be able to afford my time. I think I'm worth it but I can't deny that visiting my chambers is a rich man's hobby. Many turn up in the smartest of business suits rather than dirty rainwear, although I do see the occasional man in a raincoat. That is probably, however, because he has come to me with the specific intention of donning a raincoat as part of a fetish game. They're a popular fetish item and I keep a range in stock, in different materials and many different sizes.

The cost factor alone dictated that from the age of 20 or so onwards I was meeting much older men whose lives were all so interesting. Obviously they were mostly successful businessmen whose lives had taken them down career paths far removed from any that I might have considered. None of their jobs would have been open to a girl like me from the sort of family background from which I came. How else would I ever have interacted on an equal – or dominant – level with men who ran big businesses, or who practiced law, or who benefitted from the most expensive of public-school educations. I was a girl from a London council estate; these were a different class of people to any I might ever have met with lives that were way off my scale.

And I was not just meeting these men as you might meet them in a social situation; they were opening a window into their very souls. I see people in an intensely intimate way that they probably never reveal to their loved ones or to anyone else. I'm privy to their most coveted fantasies and fears, and possible pleasures, they have been dreaming about all of their adult lives: the secret situations and stories which they have never dared to share with their wives or their closest friends. Their most kinky and 'perverted' lusts and hidden desires. Given the importance that sex plays in all of our lives, it is like opening a door into the most intimate part of their minds.

Even further than that, I get to see both the private and the public sides of my clients. Once a man has trusted me with the secret side of the his life, once I have seen him wriggle in pain at the stroke of my riding crop, or gasp in discomfort as my entire fist slides into his arse, there is little he won't share with me. Many men want to chat about their everyday lives and relax after an orgasm has washed away the cares of their day.

For me, that recovery time is a vital part of the process. I welcome the chance to potter around tidying up equipment we might have used, coiling ropes or putting intimate toys into the steriliser, whilst still talking to my client. He or she needs time to slowly wend their way back into the 'real' world beyond my doors and I am happy to share that with them. It is astonishing what confessions they will make about their lives in those afterglow moments; I hear of their secret sexual affairs, their business decisions and their cherished hopes and plans. That is why you will never hear from my lips the real names and identities of any client who has ever passed through my door in the past 20 years. Once they get to know me, my clients know that my discretion is absolute. Just like Vegas – 'what happens in my dungeon, stays in my dungeon'.

I was learning on the job and constantly adapting my services as my client base grew. At that time of my life, still a young woman, everything was experimental and exploratory. I gathered tips and techniques from my clients all of the time: 'I want you to be stricter with me…' or, 'Please be colder and more clinical, nurse. Tell me this treatment is exactly what I need.' The variations were limited only by my clients' desires and my imagination. This was a marked departure from my earlier outcalls work. When I was dominating men in their homes or hotels I had to work a lot harder with my voice, simply because I didn't have much equipment in my travel bag. So, I would use almost exclusively verbal clues to build up the scenario my client desired. If they wanted a 'naughty schoolboy being punished' scene I would have to create the schoolroom scenario and the strict headmistress in their heads, building up the story and the fantasy in their minds until they and I were living the part together.

As soon as I had my own premises and a dungeon to work in there was no longer such a need to imagine the scenarios. I had the necessary paraphernalia to hand to bring their fantasies to life. I discovered that there was a vast range of role-plays that would turn men on. I didn't always have to scream or shout or make them crawl on the floor kissing my boots. Some men wanted a gentler, more imaginative sexual experience that I could now offer with bondage equipment, fetish clothing and creativity.

And one activity proved especially popular as time went by and my stock of clothing grew: more and more men wanted to turn into women.

CHAPTER 21

ALL GIRLS TOGETHER...

The female slave sitting patiently, tightly bound in ropes, in the corner of my room had gone to great lengths to dress to impress. An expensive designer dress was teamed with sheer, seamed stockings and an equally expensive pair of high-heeled shoes which perfectly complemented the small clutch handbag. The make-up, the eye-liner, the mascara and the lipstick were all almost perfect. Perhaps the only things out of place were the full, dark, beard and moustache and the unmistakably masculine voice as 'she' complained periodically that the ropes were too tight.

'Shut-up, Theresa,' I instructed. 'You spoil the fun by talking. Just sit there and suffer.'

Theresa, one of the first transvestite cross-dressers I played with in the early days of my career, was a very pleasant, 40-year-old, married businessman I'll call Terry. He'd booked my services several times to be dominated and humiliated before finally feeling comfortable enough with me to confess that he wanted to be dressed-up as a woman. From that point onwards he changed from Terry to Theresa. He would wear female lingerie and together we gradually accumulated a full wardrobe of women's clothing to suit his new gender assignment in our sessions. He became one of my first 'personal slaves', a privileged position in which he would still pay for sessions with me but would also be treated, once in a while, as a 'sub' on whom I could experiment with new techniques that I wanted to try out before unleashing them on my other paying clientele. It meant that Theresa was often hanging around the dungeon for hours – sometimes literally hanging around, as he was suspended in full 'en femme' costume – waiting whilst I dealt with other clients.

In his day-job, Terry ran a successful double-glazing business, managing a staff of scores of people in a factory that supplied sealed window units to some of the biggest house-builders in the country. As Theresa, his life was very different. He did all of my basic domestic chores: cleaning, tidying, polishing and taking care of the dungeon equipment as well as fetching and carrying anything I might need to keep me happy and contented. I would never chat to him as though he was a friend, because our game demanded that he stay in a submissive role whenever he was with me. Sometimes he would just sit silently in the corner waiting to be used and at other times I would try out something new that was suitably painful or humiliating. He was in his usual place in the corner on the day that I decided to spice up his life, and mine, with a little enforced bi-sexuality.

Even at that early stage of my career, I'd been asked many times for 'forced-bi' activities but was not really sure what to do. I was very inexperienced and there was nobody I could ask about it. I wasn't even sure if forced-bi had to involve penetration, or if mere oral sex would suffice. Some of my submissive, male clients would say, 'Oh, I would love to be strapped down and raped by a man' – but I had no men who wanted to do the fucking. Without an active participant I was never sure if making a man suck another man's penis would count. In the end it was actually just a case of saying to myself, 'Oh bugger it, I'll give it a go and see what happens.'

Although Terry/Theresa, like many men, enjoyed being made to dress in women's clothing I knew that he did not consider himself to be gay or bisexual and that he had no desire whatsoever for any sexual contact with other males. On this day I had another slave strapped down and helpless in the next room and so I began teasing Theresa that I was going to make him/her do new and dreadfully humiliating things. She looked more and more nervous but I told her she had a clear choice: do everything I demanded 'however humiliating, however demeaning' or leave the dungeon and never return. I was gambling on the fact that she was so addicted to our sessions that she would go along with anything rather than face her ultimate fear of being banished forever.

So I led Theresa into the next room where the other slave was already bound naked and blindfolded to my bondage bench. In my most authoritative voice, I ordered Theresa to kneel between my other sub's legs. 'Now, lick his balls,' I commanded. There was a delicious moment of silence and stillness as my words sank in. I knew that Terry, a married man who thought of himself as totally heterosexual, was struggling to come to terms with this new bisexual role I had demanded of Theresa. The thought was strangely sexually arousing for me because it was a true test of how much power I now had over this man. Could I overcome his own ingrained sexual programming to do something he truly did not want to do? It was doubly exciting because I knew that his passive and unwilling 'partner' in this game was also strictly heterosexual and would not want to have a man's tongue anywhere near his genitalia. The problem for him was that he was in no position whatsoever to object.

Needless to say, Theresa duly leaned forward and started licking; the fear of displeasing me was greater than her fear of performing an overtly homosexual act. The initial, tentative few licks soon developed, on my explicit instructions, into performing full-blown oral sex and I found that I was getting really excited as, for the first time, I watched two men together. I could see that both guys were getting a kick out of what was happening, even though it was the last thing that either of them really wanted. Neither of the men liked it and yet their bodies were betraying them with clear signs of sexual arousal. It was a new and exciting experience for both of them and that made it hugely exciting for me. I was enjoying it because they were *not* enjoying it; my excitement stemmed from the power trip of making two men do things they didn't want to do. I was the puppet-master pulling all their strings. Could that perhaps be the mark of a true dominatrix?

As it transpired, the session was a great success. We were all excited by trying something new and the two guys both clearly got off on it. Even better for me, the fact that they had been excited blew both of their minds as they calmed down at the end of the afternoon. What more could a good Mistress ask for?

Such power trips at that early stage of my career sum up what has since become my ethos in all of my sessions. I get a thrill if I know that the person isn't enjoying what I am making them do, but is still getting a kick out of it. It doesn't have to be true in every session because we are all so different from one another, but I still get a buzz from pushing limits and showing my clients things that they never believed they would be able to accept.

The sexual kicks I was experiencing from dominating men in this way made me even more determined to develop my skills as a dominatrix and to build up my business. My own sexual tastes weren't something that I could talk about with anyone; I don't think any of the girls I was friends with would have understood the thrill I was getting. Their own sex lives seemed so tame in comparison to mine. The whole concept of domination and submission was something that was barely talked about at that time and I was sure that the games I was playing were different from anything my friends might have experienced. It was just not something I could discuss.

I was also in a gentle, vanilla relationship with my then boyfriend; just straight sex with none of the domme games I was playing at work. It was creating a kind of split personality for me because I was getting all kinds of frolicky fun which I liked – but none of it was on offer at home. Even at the time I recognised that I was doing what a lot of my clients do now: compartmentalising different parts of my life and not allowing what happens in one segment to affect the other. Even more surprisingly, and although I didn't know it at the time, I would eventually go on to get caught up in a second, extremely vanilla relationship as well: all despite my recognising early on that my sexual desires were being neglected in my private life. The fun I was finding at work reinforced that feeling every day. I underwent a remarkable transformation with a month or two of having opened my dungeon for business: I was far happier, more content and less stressed than I had been in my previous 'straight' employment with the film company. I'd even lost a lot of weight that I'd piled on when dragging myself off to a job I hated each day. I knew I was looking good – and most men seemed to agree.

There was a huge contrast between the type of 'A/B' demographic men I was meeting each day – the movers and the shakers whose characters always seemed to have more than one dimension – and the far more simplistic guy I was living with at home. That may be one of the reasons why I devoted so much of my time and energy to building up the business. I was greatly enjoying my work and I was attracting people who seemed to share my tastes. I wanted to learn everything I could learn and cater for everything that interested me, and ignore the stuff that I didn't. I love rubber and found that I was drawing people into rubber sessions because that was one of my special interests.

Ultimately I believe that the reason I was successful is that to me this is not a job; I have never felt that this is a job. It's true that there are a few aspects that are like any other job: yes I have to keep accounts and I have to do paperwork, but I never feel the way that I did in any of the 'straight' jobs I've ever been involved in. In those situations there were times when I looked at the clock and thought: 'Oh God, is that the time, I have to get to work now.'

Once I had my dungeon I realised that I was having the time of my life doing what I was doing. It is still the same today: I love work and if I spend more than a week away from my office I start to miss it and want to get back. Ultimately, no matter what job you do, you have to enjoy it for the sake of your happiness and mental stability.

I was developing other new skills as well, skills which have stood me in good stead ever since. I was learning to filter out those guys whose needs were not compatible with the games I wanted to play. They are few and far between but there are some domination games from which I get no kick whatsoever. The men who want to be 'adult babies' are a case in point. I have nothing against them wanting to revert to babyhood but I always turn down such requests. I've no interest in babies – adult or otherwise. I tell them that there are plenty of other Mistresses out there on the internet who will be delighted to look after their needs. It's just not for me.

One man many years ago begged and insisted that he wanted to try watersports. The ability to piss for England being one of my many talents, I was happy to oblige. I duly tied him up and gave him the treatment he requested, at which point he went nuts, shouting and screaming and demanding to be set free. He stomped away angry that I had provided the very service he had begged to receive. As the Americans say: 'Go figure.' In fact, most of my clients adore being peed on. The gleaming, stainless-steel toilet box in the corner of my dungeon gets well used to dispense my special brand of 'house champagne' and I have long-mastered the art of dripping it, drop by drop from a syringe, into a bound slave's mouth so that he can swallow slowly without choking... unless I want him to, of course.

Remarkably few men or women clients through the years have been a problem. Very occasionally the odd guy may be seeking services I don't want to offer. They may mistakenly believe that I run an adult massage service or that I am offering the chance for them to have sexual contact with me. I usually pick this up in the initial vetting process by phone or email and I'm always very honest: 'Sorry, I think that I am not quite the one you are looking for.' Even more rarely people slip through the net and come in for a session where I think, 'Oh that really didn't work at all, for either of us.' Then I'll simply say: 'I don't think our sessions are compatible; I'm sure you will find another Mistress out there.' Most clients, however, soon became regulars. I'd even say that anyone who comes to see me eventually becomes a regular, if they can. The desire always seems to be there; it depends on how far away they live and how often they can slip away from their normal lives to visit my premises.

With the exception of the lack of romance and my preferred sex at home, things were going well in my life. I was happy in my work, my reputation was growing, the clients kept on coming, the money kept rolling in and I was indulging my passions for ever-more innovative and exciting BDSM equipment for my little dungeon. For a couple of years I still kept my eye open for another 'normal' job that might lead to a 'normal' career. I had applied to join a journalism course and had the vague idea that a job as a reporter, or a press officer, might be interesting, but the only available start date was a year ahead. By then, another year had passed and it had become harder to give up my established life and my business. I had financial commitments and overheads that a trainee journalist's salary would never have covered. The time never seemed quite right for me to jump ship and start all over again. The truth is, I didn't really want to, I was enjoying my life, there were no problems on the horizon and I was quite proud of myself.

As they say, however: 'Pride comes before a fall.'

I don't know it then, but dark clouds were already looming large on my horizon. I was about to lose those I loved most in the world and my secret life would soon be secret no more: my life was about to implode.

CHAPTER 22

AN ANNUS
HORRIBILIS

As Lady Bracknell in Oscar Wilde's *The Importance of Being Earnest* famously noted: 'To lose one parent may be regarded as a misfortune; to lose both looks like carelessness.' In which case, I'm surely one of the more careless individuals around.

I've managed to lose, in the relationship sense, my birth-mother, to never experience the love of a real father, and then to lose both adoptive parents when one died shortly after the other. To top it all, the death of my beloved grandfather was rapidly followed by splitting with Frank, my partner, *and* my best female friend – an inevitable consequence of discovering that they were not only shagging one another but also that he'd got her pregnant and offered to marry her. I think it is fair to say that this particular interlude was not the best time of my life!

Darkness descended on me in 2001 when my grandfather, the man I had always called 'Dad' and the only father figure I had ever known, was admitted to hospital. His chronic breathing problems had worsened but I and the rest of the family were confident that he would be treated and sent home, reinvigorated, for a new lease of life. That confidence was shaken when my grandmother went to visit and said she'd found dirt everywhere in his ward supposedly dedicated to the treatment of breathing disorders. 'There's dust on the floor and on almost every surface you touch,' she told me. 'How's he going to survive in there?' Dad had been in and out of hospital before, although he always preferred to have his essential steroid treatment from his local doctor at home. A return to hospital scared him, on the grounds that 'once you go in there, you don't come out'.

In the event, it was not my grandmother's dust and dirt discovery that finished Granddad off, but an unrelated bug which he encountered during his enforced hospital stay. He had already been weak when he went in, then a bug which caused stomach cramps and diarrhoea accelerated his death. In his last days, my nan and other members of the family were taking it in turns to sit by his bedside and I wanted to be there as well. I had a sort of premonition that I would be with him when he died. Because of my particular line of late-night work it was easy for me to be there in the early hours when everyone else needed to sleep. That meant that there was perhaps a certain inevitability that I was there at the last. I was in mid-sentence, chatting away to him, when he suddenly took one big, gasping breath, as though he was going to sit up, and then died.

My grandmother was at home asleep when it happened and my grandmother believed that a figure had suddenly appeared in the doorway of her bedroom. 'Johnny, is that you?' she had asked, before realising that there was nobody there. When she told me about it later I realised that the time she thought she saw her mysterious visitor coincided precisely with the time that her husband died. I had lost one of the foundation rocks of my world. My granddad's death affected me deeply and it soon became apparent that my grandmother was also unwell. I tried to help as best I could with the funeral arrangements and all of the chaos that descends on one's life after bereavement, but other troubles were fast approaching: I suspected that I was about to lose both my partner and my closest girlfriend as well.

For some time I'd recognised that my long-term partner had been acting oddly. Our relationship had never been strong, had always been based on convenience rather than deep love and passion. Now, just a few weeks after Granddad's death, it was falling apart at the seams. For years I had wanted to walk away from him, but had never been able to shake off his powerful hold over my life. I'd been terrified that my grandparents and the rest of the family might somehow hear about my secret life. My partner had never been slow to exploit my concerns and was forever warning that he would tell everyone about me if I were ever to leave him. He knew very well that I still felt guilty when I looked at my grandparents and was desperate for them never to learn the whole truth about me. I remember one occasion when we had a row and he got in his car and said he was going to tell my

221

nan that I was a prostitute. I was distraught and raced after him and saw him pull up outside of my grandparents' house. I feared the worst when my man opened the door, but the arsehole was merely teaching me a lesson. 'Hi Nan, how are you,' he said, before walking away, leaving her puzzled by his sudden concern. Once you succumb to threats there is no easy way out, and so I had stayed in the relationship far longer than I should have done.

If I am brutally honest with myself, however, I have to recognise that there was also a different kind of fear operating to tie me into the relationship. I was worried about being lonely. He was a horrible man but if you say to me, 'Why did you stay with him?' the answer is that it was stupidity, the ignorance of youth and sometimes the feeling that 'better the devil you know than the devil you don't'. I just did not think anybody else would be interested in me. I worried that any people I would want to date would not want to date me because of my lifestyle choices. I could never quite introduce the subject of what I did to any new potential partner because... well... I just couldn't do that. You have to remember that, even though this was less than two decades ago, there was a different moral compass; a very different world.

The crazy thing was that despite threatening me often to keep me by his side, I now suspected that he was the one who wanted to go. I knew he'd always fancied my closest girlfriend and now I suspected they were having an affair. My friend was short, fat, peroxide-blonde and uglier and older than me. She was also married but had told me often that she was unhappy and wanted to find somebody new. She claimed her husband was a violent man with a drinking problem, and so I realised that my partner, for all his many faults, must, for her, have seemed a very good catch. Although I was still grieving for my granddad, I knew that I had to confront them.

'Look, I know there's something between you,' I said. 'Just be honest and tell me and we'll sort it out.'

'No, no,' they insisted. 'You're not yourself, there's something wrong with you, you're just being paranoid.'

Despite their vehement and repeated denials, I could see that they were abnormally friendly. All of the signs were there. She was often at my house anyway, but now I realised how often they were together and alone whilst I was working, helping to pay his bills. As far as I was concerned, I felt that I had always been out of his league anyway, but I could see what was happening and that both of them were lying to my face, telling me that I was paranoid and trying to make me think I was going mad and having some kind of breakdown. When I asked them again, he got really aggressive and she started shouting her mouth off at me. In the middle of my grief, they actually had me thinking, 'Am I actually that paranoid? Is it me, am I imagining things?' Deep down, however, I knew that wasn't true.

Things came to a head when she asked me to write a reference for a new flat in order that she could leave her husband. Despite my suspicions I helped her out but then she was sketchy and evasive about to where exactly she was moving. The next thing was that Frank offered to help her move because she didn't have a car. That's just what he was supposedly doing one night when he stayed out late into the evening. I just thought, 'Well, where the fuck is he? He hasn't come home and I've no idea where she's living.' So I got in my car and I took in a few streets, just following my nose as though some sort of instinct was directing me. Just a half-a-mile away I found Frank's car parked outside of a block of flats.

They must have seen me draw up and park in the street because she and Frank suddenly appeared in the doorway together.

'What the fuck is going on?' I cried. 'What are you doing here?' I was upset, angry and in no mood to be pissed around any longer. There was an angry confrontation on the doorstep with him getting mad, her getting mad and me demanding some answers. Eventually, she let me into the house and dropped the bombshell I had never expected: 'I'm pregnant... with Frank's baby... we're going to get married.'

It was a body blow made worse by the discussions Frank and I had often had about children. He had been married before and had had two kids with his wife. He always insisted that he didn't want to even consider having more children for the moment, not least because I was having to constantly help him out financially by contributing to his child maintenance payments. He talked vaguely of the possibility of children in the future, but not until his first family had grown up and were no longer a financial liability. I had not really wanted children myself at that stage but I always thought my views might mellow in the future. Every time I had pressed him about it he had made it clear that kids were pretty much off the cards; one more thing to add to his long list of lies and deceit.

To suddenly be told that not only were they getting married but also that she was pregnant was a knife-wound to my heart; it really, really hurt.

'How can you have hidden something like that?' I said. 'I've asked you over and over if you're seeing Frank behind my back… and now you tell me you're pregnant.'

'We didn't have a choice,' she claimed. 'You would have kicked Frank out and we didn't have anywhere to go. We needed to get this flat first before we told you anything. Now we're going to live together. We're getting married, having the baby… blah, blah, blah.'

I could hardly listen to their explanations; I was devastated and had run out of things to say to try and make then see how much they had hurt me. Deeply upset, I headed home, leaving them alone in the flat I had helped them to rent and with the car I had helped him to buy because he couldn't afford the repayments. I had barely got home when her husband phoned me.

He was upset too but had no idea of the truth of what had been happening. She had told him she wanted a divorce but had lied to him by saying that there was no other man involved. She had claimed she 'wanted some space from him' and needed to live on her own. The truth is that he had been due to inherit some family money and she had wanted the divorce to go through amicably in order that she could collect a share of the money that was coming to him.

The idea of her fooling both her husband and me was too much to bear; something snapped inside and pure, white-hot revenge poured out of me.

'Just so you know,' I said. 'She's not just leaving you, she's moving in with Frank, she's pregnant… it's his child… they're getting married – and this is where they're living.'

I can't defend myself by lying about the reasons why I did

it. Frank had taken the piss out of me; he'd been lying to me for years; he'd been leaching money from me for years. She was my best friend who had stolen my partner, had fucked him in my house, had lied through her teeth and got herself pregnant. On top of that, the man I knew as my dad had just died and they took advantage of my confusion to make their escape. How much worse could it get? What else could they possibly do to me? By the time he left I hadn't loved him for years but being shafted like that still hurt me badly. My words now were pure revenge, a woman scorned, jealousy, sadness and rage all rolled into one vitriolic ball. You bet I told her husband all about it.

But there was no sweetness in getting my revenge, when my own life was turned upside down through someone leaking news of my professional lifestyle to my family. To say that the news didn't go down well with my birth-mother is perhaps the understatement of the year. All I can remember about what proved to be a truly terrible few days was that she repeatedly called me up, bawling her eyes out, crying so much she couldn't even speak. 'What about your education,' she gasped. 'What about your degrees… you've got two degrees… are you still looking for work… how could you do this for a living?'

I tried to explain that I wasn't actually guilty as charged: I had a website but it was for domination services, not for prostitution. Prostitutes have sex with men for money, I didn't do that. I just bossed men around, beat them a little, humiliated them if that's what they wanted; they never got to touch my body. But nothing that I said made the slightest difference. She was just devastated. She had just lost her father and had then been hit with news about her daughter.

'Oh Miranda… do you touch men's willies?' she sobbed: it seemed that was all she wanted to know.

The only saving grace was that between us all we somehow managed to keep the revelation from my grandmother's ears. My family didn't need to keep the secret much longer. Whether or not her husband's death took away my nan's will to live, it was not long afterwards that she succumbed to pancreatic cancer. Whereas my grandfather had passed away relatively peacefully, my nan didn't have a good death. She had lost loads of weight and had become jaundiced before they admitted her to hospital. She lingered for weeks and I visited her regularly, doing silly things like painting her nails to try and keep her spirits up. But the cancer had by then spread to her lungs and there was no hope of recovery. Once again, because of my peculiar working hours, I was with her when she died. She had been begging for pain relief and was deeply distressed and trying to climb out of bed because she was in such discomfort. It was an awful experience to see her die that way. Even though I had long before moved out of their house, my nan and my grandfather were the only parents I had ever known and their deaths left a terrible void in my life. It was dreadful to have to go and help clean out their house – the little, unheated council house where I had spent my childhood, now empty and even more unloved without them. I was still in regular, close contact with my birth-mother but she was no substitute for my nan and granddad: I had lost my parents.

Meanwhile, in time – quite a lot of time actually – my birth-mother recovered from the shock of learning about my lifestyle and stopped crying every time we spoke. I had to do a lot of re-education of all my family, teaching them the difference between my work as a dominatrix and the work of a prostitute. Some of them got it, some of them didn't, but I did my best to smooth over the ruffled feathers. Explaining the contents of my internet website helped a little – but these were not great conversations to have.

In 1992, Her Majesty the Queen famously declared the year had been an *annus horribilis* when, among other calamities, fire destroyed part of Windsor Castle. Well, please excuse my language but, in my more down-to-earth world, I think of this period of my life as having come up against an *anus* horribilis, thanks to my toe-rag, wank-stain of a partner who right-royally shafted my arse that year. He brought me pain, unhappiness and caused me to shed a lot of tears. And yet, he and my treacherous girlfriend did me a favour. After years of a loveless relationship, full of the fear of exposure, I was finally free; my family now knew what I did; I wasn't ashamed of my job; and a life finally free of worry was stretching out before me.

CHAPTER 23

FINDING
MY FATHER

I might finally have been free of my unwanted partner but I was still suffering from the after effects of months of emotional turmoil.

Relations with my birth-mother were still traumatic and my beloved nan and granddad had gone. I had financial worries because of the legacy left by my unfaithful and unreliable former other half. He had promised to take care of the repayments on his own car, but never actually paid a penny. Because I had helped him fund the vehicle I found myself getting demands for overdue payments for a car I didn't own. In the end I had no choice but to tell the company to repossess it. That added to the outstanding bill and ruined my own credit rating for a while. We had recently moved into a house and Frank had left building work undone all over the property. He had charged me for doing the work but never completed the project.

It was a pretty dark time. I had lost a lot of weight and was having dreams about suicide; not that I would ever do it, but it seemed to be a way of my mind subconsciously coping with what I had been through. I kept dreaming I was going into my own dungeon, now built in the garage, and hanging myself. My dreams would play through different scenarios as though my mind were exploring different ways that events would unfold. And always at the end of each one I would end up throwing a rope around my neck and stringing myself up from the rafters. Fortunately I had no such feelings when I was awake, in fact I had few feelings at all; I was just numb. In this slightly surreal state of mind, when things were racing around in my head and I had nobody to talk to, a new idea crystallised in my mind: I would find my real father.

I had never known anything about my real father. My grandmother had destroyed my birth certificate, although I still do not know to this day if his name appears on the official record of my birth. The immediate catalyst for setting out on my search had been finding an old toy whilst clearing out my late grandparents' house. After my birth-mother left home, I had been their only child, the only one they might have bought presents for, and there in the attic was a toy I'd never seen before – an unused, pristine-condition, skateboard. It was hard to imagine my wheezing old granddad or grandmother being secret skate-boarding enthusiasts and so the discovery was a puzzle.

When I asked my birth-mother about it, a few tantalising facts emerged about my father. Apparently he kept in touch with me for almost a year, but my grandparents had discouraged him from maintaining any contact. The skateboard had been his present to me when I was very young, a present totally inappropriate for my age. Eileen said that she could remember it being around the house for a few days but that it had then suddenly vanished. She was shocked to see it again, having been convinced that my grandparents had destroyed it and any other links with my father. Apparently she had also given them lots of things like the name tags from my wrist when I was born and my first baby bootees, but my nan had preferred to destroy all traces of my earliest days. It was not the first time that Eileen had told me things about my father and she had always told me I could ask her whatever I wished. But I had always felt uncomfortable thinking about him in any way; perhaps all a part of my childish desire to bury the slight puzzles and oddities of my life in a way that allowed me never to look at the truth. Now that my grandparents were gone, perhaps it was time to find the man who had sired me?

I honestly can't remember exactly how I got in contact. I knew that his parents had lived almost opposite my grandparents' home and so I probably just looked them up in the phone book. By chance he was living in his parents' old home because his mother had recently been taken into care. So it was just coincidence that when I phoned the house he was there and he picked up the phone.

'Hello, is that Gordon?'

'Yes,' he replied.

'It's Miranda here, your daughter'

'I can't believe it, I can't believe it,' he said. 'I never ever thought they'd told you who I was. I can't believe that you've phoned me.'

In the conversation that followed he did pretty much all of the talking. He told me that he'd often wanted to contact me but hadn't known if I would know who he was. He was happy that I called, very happy. He suggested that we meet and I agreed, purely because I was intrigued to find out what he was like. Even so, I was reserved and a little cautious because it all felt far too late in my life for this to be happening. The one thing that I was certain of is that I was not seeking somebody to replace my grandparents but I'd already decided before I made the call that we would have to meet. I simply needed to satisfy the curiosity about him that had been there for much of my life. As soon as I'd discovered in my childhood that his parents lived over the road I'd wondered if he or they ever thought about me or watched me out and about in the street. I had all these things in my head thinking: 'Has he sat there and watched me grow up; have I ever spoken to him and not realised?' I wondered if he had ever seen me out with my friends, or on nights when I might have been having a laugh and a drink in the pub. I would never have known if he was watching me because I would never have known who to look for, if that makes sense.

I finally met my father in a near-empty pub. He got us both a drink and we sat down together and chatted. Again, he did most of the talking because I didn't really have any burning questions to ask him. I was just curious and wanted to draw a line under a few things that had always puzzled me. He, on the other hand, had lots that he wanted to say to me. I think he had a lot of guilt inside him because he seemed bursting with enthusiasm to plead his case that he had really wanted to see me but had always been warned away.

'You know I was told not to go anywhere near,' he kept saying. 'I made attempts to contact you but everything was shut down from your grandparents' end. I kept being told they wanted zero contact, what could I do?'

I didn't tell him at the time but I was thinking how weak, how very weak and feeble he sounded.

'Why didn't you argue back?' I was thinking. 'You say you wanted me to know you, but you never really tried at all. How could you have just stood back and let them defeat you like that, how could you be so incredibly weak?'

The only thing stopping me from speaking out was that I knew he had been very young at the time and had problems of his own. I had learned enough from Eileen to know that he had never really been suitable parent material and was always letting her down whilst they were together.

He told me of his travels to other countries where he had lived for much of his life and, over the course of a three-hour meeting he asked me repeatedly about my life and my career. I lied and told him that I worked as a beauty therapist, my stock reply for anyone who wanted to know how I earned my living. He kept on asking whether I thought I was a 'pioneer' or a 'settler': did I like to explore the world and avoid a nine-to-five existence, or was I happy to be normal and put down strong roots? I think he was proud to think of himself as a pioneer who travelled the world and didn't live a dull and predictable life and wanted to know if I was a chip off the old block. I so wanted to tell him how unusual and non-nine-to-five my own life truly was, but I didn't have the heart to shock him. Instead I told him that yes, I loved exploring the world but ultimately I needed my own home, a stable base. He had no need to know that I was a busy and increasingly successful dominatrix – *that* knowledge could come later. We parted amicably enough and I agreed to meet him again. He was looking after his mother's old house whilst she was in care and wanted me to go over and meet his wife and family. I gathered that he had a step-daughter, his wife's daughter, whom he had helped to raise.

In due course I did meet his family and couldn't help but think: 'He's had time to help raise another man's daughter – but no time ever for his own.'

Even so, I asked him to visit my house. I decided that it was time for honesty to prevail and that I should tell him the truth about my dominatrix career. That meeting was possibly never destined to go well: he was a born-again Christian.

With my real father sitting in my house, I told him some of the tragic events that had overtaken me in the past few months. My grandparents' death, my partner's betrayal and the fact that my birth-mother would not now stop crying because she had been told I was a prostitute. It was, I suppose, a lot to take in at one time and I could see that he was shocked.

'Of course, I'm not a prostitute but I do work in the sex industry,' I said. I explained that things were a bit strained within what was left of my family environment because of this explosion of information coming out unexpectedly. I knew by then that he considered himself to be a born-again Christian with strong religious beliefs but I wasn't quite prepared for his reaction.

'Oh, I sense a great darkness around you, there are dark forces surrounding you,' he intoned. 'You have got choices in life and I see that you are going to the dark side.'

I could feel myself getting annoyed as he wombled on about 'dark forces' as though I was somehow in the grip of demonic possession. He seemed to be suggesting that he really should keep his distance because of the darkness around me. And I thought, 'Well yeah, I am feeling a bit dark at the moment – probably because I just lost my grandfather, my partner, things aren't really going too well in my family because of what the arsewipe told them and so, yeah, I may be coming across as a little bit pessimistic but, you know what, that's not really surprising, is it?'

I couldn't keep my darker thoughts about him out of my head any longer. I was thinking: 'Fuck off, fuck off, you weirdo, right now back to Australia'. What I actually said to him was: 'Screw you; who are you to judge me in any way. How dare you say things like that? Who the fuck are you to stand there, someone who hasn't seen me in like 21 years, and you're telling me that I am surrounded by dark forces? I'm not fucking interested!'

As you can probably tell, I was actually pretty annoyed by that stage. A bloody born-again Christian was the last thing I needed in my life right then!

'How can you preach about fucking forgiveness as a Christian and then tell me this after you have not even been bothered with me for how many years? Fuck off.'

The resultant row was short, sharp and nasty with the upshot being that I told him exactly where he could stick his Christian beliefs and that once he'd done that he should never contact me again.

That's been pretty much the last contact I ever had with my real father. He did write to me afterwards with what seemed to be an apology, saying that he had been affected by his mother's illness and that it had been a shock to see me and learn of my work. 'Things were said in the heat of the moment,' he said, 'but I would like to contact you again.'

I sent an email back saying: 'Thank you for your apology; I can accept it but I can't really forgive how you made me feel at what you must have known was the worst time of my life. So you are not going to meet me again. Please don't contact me again. I've no interest in knowing you.'

I could accept that he probably had his own issues to cope with at the time we met but he was supposed to be the mature, responsible adult and he handled it all so badly. He said all the wrong things to me after he had years to think of all the right things to say.

'I really don't need somebody else putting me down right now,' I thought. 'The last thing I need is to feel rejected by somebody else in my life.'

We've never spoken since.

CHAPTER 24

SORRY GUYS...
SIZE MATTERS

I had bought the most expensive, luxury lingerie especially for the occasion and I knew that I was looking good. I was dressed only in a black bra and sheer black panties, standing by the bed in an anonymous hotel room and waiting for sex on demand.

Displaying himself naked in front of me was a handsome hunk of a man: tall, dark-haired, muscular, exceptionally well-endowed and sporting an erection fit to burst. I was feeling horny, excited, moist, and as nervous as a virgin schoolgirl on her first date. The reason for the butterflies flapping around in my tummy was not just the prospect of imminent intercourse with a male body most women would die for. It was the fact that this was no ordinary date and, until a few moments earlier in the hotel bar, I had never met the guy who was about to fuck me.

237

This was a man I had selected only after the most careful study of scores of possible candidates. I was paying for this night of casual sex and I fully intended to get my money's worth.

'Lie down on the bed and be quiet,' I instructed. 'Just do your job and stay hard while I ride you.'

Expertly slipping a condom over his rock-hard cock, I knelt over his body, lowered myself into position and gasped with pleasure as I felt for myself just how well-hung this man really was. Hiring a male escort for the evening had not been cheap but the multiple orgasms he was about to give me would make this the bargain of the century...

But first I need to explain how I had reached that point in my life.

The irony of a professional dominatrix paying a man to make love to her was not lost on me. It had taken me a long while to pluck up the courage to start searching the internet for a suitable gigolo and then even more courage to make the call. The decision came after almost three years of a totally sexless relationship. To put it bluntly: I hadn't been fucked in ages and my frustration levels were bubbling over to bursting point.

I am, however, jumping ahead in my story once more. My pressing need for a gigolo only arose at the end of another long relationship into which I had bounced, unthinkingly, after my break-up with Frank. It was a classic mistake, an attraction on the rebound from a disastrous affair. Just a few months after my partner and my best friend ran off with each other I walked mindlessly into yet another relationship which failed almost as soon as it had started. In my own defence I can only say that I was still trying to rebuild my life after the series of emotional disasters that had befallen me and which had, I suppose, left me alone and vulnerable. The damage with which I was coping was not just emotional. My former partner had left my house and my working dungeon in the garage in a state of disrepair. Half-finished plumbing and DIY work and no man to tackle the task. My domination business was back on track and I had enough money coming in to pay for the work, but it was hard to find a trader whom I could trust.

I was still good friends with a girl I'd worked with at the film equipment hire company. She was one of the few 'straight' people I had ever told about my secret sexy role and she was fascinated by my life. She came round to my house on one occasion and was bowled over by my collection of corsets and boots and glamorous wigs. She wanted to try on all my clothes and examine all of my elaborate bondage and torture equipment. She loved it all.

Now, she suggested a solution to my problem. She recommended her husband's friend, James. He was a builder of sorts, he was out of work, and he was willing to work for whatever I could afford to pay. The first time he came to my house to assess what needed to be done I vaguely registered that he wasn't bad looking but there was as far as my feelings went. After recent events I was numb, emotionally bruised and totally immune to the charms of any man. In fact the only men I was seeing were the clients who came to my dungeon, my chamber of delights built into the garage in the garden at the back of the house.

After years of a miserable and loveless relationship, James proved to be a breath of fresh air. Once he started work on the house I realised that he was incredibly easy-going, laid-back and very chilled. After a long time being tied to a tosser who was precisely the opposite, always uptight and manipulative, it was a delight to meet a man with a ready smile and a good sense of humour. We got on fine but I still don't quite know how we ended up as lovers. I hardly drank, but James was a typical builder with a thirst for a few beers at the end of the working day. With the money I paid him, he used to pop down the road and buy half a dozen beers which he would drink whilst he was working. On one Friday night we ended up sharing the beers and, somehow, got a little closer than I'd planned. By the end of the evening we had fallen into bed together. I don't think the sex was particularly memorable but after a long period of celibacy it was good enough for me to want to carry on. Within a week or two we were together full time; it was not so much that he moved in with me, it was more that he couldn't be bothered to go home any longer.

I was once again back in a steady relationship with a man who was happy to share my bed and who didn't mind that I was meeting other men all day long in my guise as Mistress Miranda. James was probably the least jealous man I had ever known and, although he knew all about my work, he didn't mind in the slightest. My particular brand of sexual excitement wasn't, however, to his tastes. I knew that he thought the whole BDSM work was slightly strange. And I was back in the routine of kinky games with lots of men, and the occasional woman, and strictly vanilla sex with my partner at night. What was it about me? I thought. How can I be the way I am, a sex goddess and cruel mistress to so many clients, and yet keep on attracting these vanilla men? It was like some form of curse was upon me, never to find the ideal package all in one guy.

For the first six months or maybe a year, all was fine. Then James and I gradually started arguing more and more. I don't know, yet again, why we stayed together. There were plenty of times I determined to throw him out but never quite got around to making him go. I guess that yet again I settled for convenience and 'better the devil you know'. Life with him had become dull and argumentative but he was always promising that he would pull himself together and that things would get better for both of us. I suppose there was also a secret fear that I might not find another man willing to accept my unusual line of work and that my self-confidence was still battered by the horrors of my last relationship. Whatever the reason, we drifted along in a state of argumentative unhappiness with neither of us willing to finally pull the plug. Somehow, years had suddenly slipped by, many of them with no sex between us at all.

It wasn't that I was keeping score on the bedhead or anything, but the day dawned when I could no longer remember the last time that my partner and I had made love. A little thought pinned down the problem more clearly: we hadn't had sex for a year-and-a-half. For two fit and healthy people in their early thirties, this was ridiculous! I set about persuading James that sex would be a great idea, but I was fighting an uphill battle; he was probably the most sexless man I had ever known. It took more than a month of constant nagging and even the threat that I might start to look elsewhere before James managed to fuck me again. For the briefest of whiles all seemed to be back on track, but it was a further year-and-a-half before we tried it again. I couldn't go on being excited each day by clients, with whom I wouldn't want to have sex, and being frustrated all night lying next to a man who didn't want to fuck me. A woman – as they say – has needs. Something had to give.

In the end I gave James his marching orders. There was no other man in my life, no other man on the horizon but I no longer wanted James in my bed. He moved out – but only as far as the spare room. This guy was so laid back that he couldn't be bothered to find a new place and was determined to cling on to his place in my home. For months after we had agreed to split up he hung around like a bad smell. He even refused to tell his family and our mutual friends that we were no longer together. My family already knew, because I had told them straight that we had split up. But James kept pleading, 'Oh no, I'll tell my family when the time is right – later, later', anything to put off facing the reality of our situation. I began to think that I would have to live forever with this zombie from a now-dead relationship; nothing I could do would make him lie down and die. Even while I was tackling that issue, I was also deeply aware of another seemingly intractable problem. My sex life was still non-existent. Something had to be done.

The idea of searching for a hunky male escort had been rolling around in my fantasy life for some time. I know that the idea of paying for sex shocks many women but you have to remember the type of world I inhabited. My days were spent in the dungeon where business was booming and everyone I

242

met was kinky and fun and fascinating in one way or another. I had started a website of my own, advertising my services as 'The Bondage Mistress.com' and had also begun filming some of my escapades to sell the clips online or in a specially created private site for paying members only.

As with all of my new business ventures, I started from scratch with none of the specialist knowledge I needed and learned as fast as I could. Because I had not the faintest idea how to set up and run a website, I employed a man who did. It was an inauspicious start because he was obsessed with 'swingers' clubs and knew little of my totally different world of BDSM. I kept finding links on my site to swinging activities and then realised that he was writing utterly inappropriate text on my site, describing me as 'Mistress Miranda: To be Feared and Obeyed'. It was nowhere near the image I wanted to portray and nowhere near the style of BDSM play which I wanted to follow. Many dominatrices present a fearsome face to the world. They trade on being harsh and strict and cruel to their clients, demanding that men cower on the floor in front of them and screaming at their slaves to gain instant obedience. Many men like that harsher treatment and I am the first to say 'good luck' to them, 'whatever turns you on'. That has never been my style, however. I prefer a more civilised training regime, strict and extreme bondage, rarely raising my voice and able to put a slave in his or her place with a naughty smile on my face. Now the guy who was creating my website was turning me into everything I had never wanted to be.

A change of web manager later and my site started bringing in new income from my films and members' club, as well as serving as an ideal advertising forum for my session services.

Things were back on track with my business, but I was still sex-starved. Having turned to the internet to build up my career, it was only natural that I should use it again for more personal purposes – a far more personal service. I began searching the web for a suitable male escort. From the start I knew exactly what I wanted. This was not to be a romance; I didn't want a lifelong-partner, or even some fancy form of dinner-date. I wanted to be shagged, preferably shagged hard, ideally, shagged senseless.

Finding a man to do that was not as easy as you might think. The web search turned up site after site, each packed full of pictures of hunky young men. Unfortunately, all of them were gay. Now, I have nothing whatsoever against gay men – or gay women – for that matter. Many of my days in the dungeon are spent with guys playing forced bisexual games or with women who expose their bodies to be explored, probed and tormented by me in front of the cameras. Some of my fellow dommes, many of them my closest friends and work colleagues, are happily gay or bi-sexual. It is just not *my* thing; straight men turn me on in the way a woman never could. I wanted a red-blooded, totally heterosexual man who could perform to order, with me being the centre of his undivided sexual attention. I returned to my search.

My decision to buy myself some instant sex was not an instant one. I'd deliberated about it for ages, letting the idea mature and then flipping on to different internet sites, exciting myself by picking out the pictures of my ideal candidates. It was a form of fascinating self-stimulation over which I was determined to take my time and enjoy to the full. Yet although

I was having a whale of a time, a little part of me was clinging on to normality. A tiny bit of my brain was thinking: 'Oh God, you know, what has my life come to?' whilst a much bigger part was thinking, 'Wow, this is great. I'm a kid let loose in a sweetie shop, trawling through these sites.'

This was going to be my first sexual adventure in ages; it had to be with somebody exciting —and it had to be good. Eventually I found what I had been looking for: some straight escorts whose naked photographs showed that they had all of the necessary accoutrements to meet my demands. I had set the bar deliberately high and many fell at the first hurdle: too short, too thin, too blond, not muscular enough, or not hand-some enough. All of these faults were grounds for instant rejection. And that, of course, was even before we came to the penises. Comparing those was a tough job, but, as they say, somebody had to do it.

Eventually, and after many hours of selfless study, I picked the lucky man. 'Yes,' I thought, 'this is the one. The most perfect person I can find to fuck me.'

My choice did have a lot going for him. He was younger than me, but not too young. He was a fitness model and had a perfect body; he had the looks, the height and was ridiculously handsome. The website didn't show off his most important attribute in its fully erect state, but what could be seen was more than impressive... 'Probably,' I thought, 'as much as I can handle.' This was going to be fun. To double check that I was not deluding myself and buying a pig in a poke, I shared my choice with one of my closest female friends. She breathlessly agreed that he was an amazing specimen of a man; a definite seal of approval.

I thought, 'Fuck it, I have had a miserable time, I want to feel sexy again, I want to feel special.' I mean, I knew that my clients found me desirable and all the rest of it, but I just wanted that extra little buzz. So, yeah I booked him – and it was great.

We met at a hotel, and what can I say? My nerves were jangling as I waited for him to appear. I can't even tell you how hideously nervous I was; it was just not like me at all. Here I was, the ultimate, confident dominatrix, the famous Mistress Miranda, and I was shaking like a leaf. I guess part of me thought he wouldn't show up, part of me was scared that he would and I didn't know quite which way I wanted it to go. It was very strange for me to be on the other side of the coin for once: selecting someone and arranging to meet them in the way that my clients must feel when they first choose me for a visit.

In the event, the evening went on for hours but seemed to fly by in an instant. The sex was every bit as fantastic as I had hoped it would be: raw, visceral, pounding and hard. It turned out that I had been incredibly lucky with the guy that I had chosen and the whole thing was fantastic. I took charge of the way we made love and found that hugely exciting. This was orgasmic sex at its best, it definitely hit double figures; what more could a woman ask for?

CHAPTER 25

WEST LONDON TOWERS

I can't now quite remember whether or not my gigolo awayday came before or after I moved my entire business operation to its current home. I fondly refer to my premises as 'West London Towers' with its appealing overtones of a somewhat eccentric, British stately home. It is in fact a cosy, yet spacious, suburban house with multiple playspaces on multiple floors. It is ideally fit for its purpose, a quiet and discreet hideaway for tormenting and binding my slaves in uninterrupted, soundproofed and lonely luxury.

I now live elsewhere in London but the same house remains the nerve-centre of what has become something of an international business operation, regularly taking me out of the country to Europe and the USA for filming trips or to make and maintain contacts with other dominatrices and adult film production companies.

The filming company I now own is an important part of my commercial operation, but still at the heart of what I do are the intimate sessions with selected personal clients. That has little changed over the years. Anyone can book a domination session with me; the delay in getting an appointment may these days be a little longer than once it was, but I remain totally committed to the heartbeat of my business.

The gradual growth of my commercial success came once I fully realised the power of advertising. In the early days of my dungeon I gained clients through leaving my cards in local brothels and by advertisements in local, weekly newspapers. Most of the guys who came to see me were from perhaps a 25-mile radius around my home. Then I discovered that I could place ads in *Exchange and Mart* magazine which has a far wider readership and brought in clients from all over the UK. The biggest change, however, came with my starting to advertise in international magazines that specialised in articles and pictures of dominant women. It was a major expense but rapidly changed the nature of my client base. These glossy, expensive publications circulated amongst a different kind of client all over the world. Their readers were men, and some-times couples, who were deeply committed to and involved in the fetish world. And they came from all over.

My premises are not far from London's main international airport, Heathrow, and with its easy transport access I started to get more clients from abroad, particularly America. These were mostly powerful businessmen, visiting London for their companies but fascinated by the fetish world and wealthy enough to be able to indulge their special interests with me.

There have been other changes over the years. I once

worked in a lonely and isolated bubble of kinkiness in a garage at the rear of my home; I now have the space and the experience to offer astonishing new experiences to my eager clients. Either for a filming shoot, or often just for fun, I can be found 'double-domming' with a dominatrix colleague, or teasing a hapless and frustrated male with the delights of one of my stable of available young slavegirls. Foremost among these is my sexy young submissive, the beautiful and oh-so-compliant Miss Sherry. She's naughty, feisty, unruly and badly behaved. I frequently have to punish her for cheekiness and for teasing my male slaves as soon as my back is turned. I would not, however, want to be without her. She is one of my closest confidantes and friends.

I met Sherry many years ago through a mutual friend in the BDSM scene who knew what I did for a living. On several occasions I'd mentioned to her my need for a submissive girl and asked her to pass on my number to anyone who might be interested in working with me. The result was a meeting with Sherry, then a petite young student with whom I immediately struck up a firm friendship that has lasted till this day. We found we had a lot in common: she was at university and seeking work in the 'adult' world to fund her studies and was thinking of taking a job in a brothel. Sherry enjoys sex, enjoys meeting new men and has the most delightful, calm and pleasing manner imaginable. She hadn't found the escort work she wanted but was clearly keen to get started. She was highly intelligent but, although she was studying for a law degree, I immediately thought that the description 'ditzy' would fit her to perfection. Sherry made it clear that she would be only too happy to audition for a new role as a slavegirl in my fast-growing business. Even as we spoke I had the ideal client in mind to introduce her to my world. He was a regular visitor who loved the idea of being sexually teased and repeatedly denied. As I have never allowed any sexual contact between the clients and myself, I needed a willing girl to drive him crazy with her body before I introduced an element of discipline and denial into the proceedings. On his next visit, I made his dreams come true and took him to visit Sherry in a hotel room nearby.

Ideally from my point of view, both the client and Sherry were happy to be filmed at play, and so the room got a little more crowded as my cameraman was added into the mix. I don't think either the guy or Sherry even noticed the camera as she threw herself into the role of sexy siren to drive his frustration levels through the roof. She touched him, let him touch her breasts and pussy, and even decided she should sit on his face to give him a taste of her feminine charms. Every time I thought he was having a little bit too much fun and that he might lose control and prematurely bring proceedings to a halt, I was on hand to ensure that a little pain brought him back down to earth with a bump. I could see immediately that Sherry was a natural and the perfect submissive bundle to add into my operation. She was friendly, fun and sexy; she was most definitely not into receiving serious pain herself, but was totally happy to sit on a client's face without her knickers on – a regular request from many of my customers who know they'll never get that service from me.

Sherry was, in fact, everything I could have desired. Most importantly, she had not been doing this kind of work for long and was not in the slightest bit jaded. She was a real bundle of laughs, and really got into the role play. She and I hit it off straightaway and agreed then and there to make another film or two together in my chambers. A week or so later, Sherry turned up at my door, ready to become a star of the silver screen as I introduced her to all of the wonders of room after room of bondage and domination equipment. Sherry admitted that she was kinky in the extreme and enjoyed the whole idea of bondage, so seeing my equipment was a mega eye-opener for her. She just went around saying, 'Wow, I can't believe this, look at this stuff, oh my God.' She was just completely over-whelmed and interested and excited and titillated and with a genuine desire to know more.

Sherry came in for a session with the same client she'd already met and we produced a film entitled *Sherry Trifle*. Okay, perhaps not the most imaginative title in the film lexicon, but it made me laugh. I laid her down naked, strapped her to the bondage bench and let him cover her with fruit, cream and other messy foodstuffs. In retrospect I should perhaps have taken the jug of custard out of the fridge *before* we poured it onto her body, but at least it woke her up. The deal was that he then got to eat all the food from this unique human plate – and he did find plenty of places to put soft fruit and a banana. I can't imagine why he found that enjoyable... Personally I would just have scoffed down the food without bothering with the sexual arousal – but then I am always hungry and even the lovely Sherry can't turn me on to personal play with women.

Watching the film back recently on my archive site, I was struck by just how much Sherry enjoyed its production. Despite being covered in cold custard, chocolate buttons and cherries – or more likely *because* she was covered in cold custard, chocolate buttons and cherries – she giggled her way through the entire event, and still managed to look, sound and feel sexy. The film reached a climax, literally, when the client got so excited that I decided a little cooling off was required. I positioned myself strategically over his face and poured out a flood of my highly-personal house champagne over him and my slavegirl. As he reached his damp, warm watersport climax I glanced down at Sherry to find her touching her vagina and still stroking his cock to expertly milk out his pleasure. Sherry was still smiling; I knew that a star was born. This girl was a natural.

Soon after that I introduced my new slavegirl to the delights of her own bondage session. This time I tested out the limits of Sherry's own submission. I discovered that she, like many of my male slaves, gets her own sexual kick from doing all that she can to please me. She was not really into severe pain but loved me putting her in bondage and being masterful to make her accept whatever suffering I wanted to impose. I was relatively kind but still clamped her nipples tightly enough to make her squeal, applied some stinging electrics and spanked her pert little behind to a satisfying, rosy glow.

Ever since then, Sherry has proved to be a firm favourite with my clients, despite her cheeky habit of trying to get her fellow slaves into trouble whenever I'm not paying attention. Many a client has found himself being punished by me because Sherry has been naughty behind my back and playfully blamed it on him. *Caveat Emptor*: clients who purchase her services will find their nipples will be fair game to be squeezed as soon as I'm out of the room and they will find themselves accused of naughtiness they knew nothing about. Not, of course, that pleas of innocence of any crime will cut any ice with me if Sherry complains. They'll still be punished. I don't allow my clients to give orders to Sherry, she is only submissive to me; but there's little she won't do if I order her obedience.

In fact, it has become obvious over the years that Sherry enjoys the sessions almost as much as do my clients. Her orgasms are never faked; sometimes a bit noisy and with a tad too much squealing for my own tastes, but never faked. And she shows a delightful acceptance of any situation in which I might put her. I remember on one occasion stripping both her and one of my male slaves butt-naked and forcing them together into an all-enveloping, rubber body bag. I zipped up the bag so that they were immovably pressed against each other within the tight and dark confines of the heavy latex covering. It was a situation that many would have found claustrophobic and distressing but when I felt they had suffered enough and unzipped the rubber package I found that Sherry had simply drifted off to sleep. She had experienced and shared the 'floaty' pleasure that so many of my men get from tight rubber bondage.

There has been just one area of my bondage Mistress activities where Sherry has so far failed to shine. In recent times I've encouraged her try being a dominant herself, letting her act as my assistant in some scenes. It's not been an easy task to draw out the dominant side of her personality. On one occasion I dressed her in a rubber catsuit and instructed her to 'look mean'. She instantly took on the appearance of a lost little lamb: 'I just don't know what to do, I don't know what to do,' she pleaded. The photographer whom I had hired especially was laughing so much that the shoot was a disaster. Perhaps one is either born to be a bondage Mistress, or not.

Our friendship has spread beyond the workplace into our personal lives, although the age gap between us means that out shared love of fine food is one of our few common interests outside of the dungeon. We have, however, grown closer from taking several filming trips abroad together and from being booked by one regular client to stay together with him in a luxury hotel on the continent. The overnight trip always follows a similar pattern: he enjoys both Sherry and I accompanying him for dinner and then loves watching as I abuse her body in his hotel room afterwards. I should confess that I can, on occasions, be mean to poor Sherry. There have been times when she's had a cock-gag strapped into her mouth and been tied too close for comfort to a man's body, and other occasions when the electrics may have been turned up a little higher than she deserved – all totally accidentally on my part, of course. I would never just pick up a cane and give her the sort of treatment that I might give a man but perhaps a flogging might take her to her limits or the nipple clamps will be a little harsher than usual.

Sherry is but one of a group of several slavegirls, some of them professional submissives and some of them keen amateur masochists, who work with me on a regular basis. More frequently, however, you are likely to find me playing host to a visiting dominatrix from elsewhere in the UK, from Europe or even over on a tour from the USA. Playing with two Mistresses and one hapless slave can be the greatest fun and

I'm always delighted to both learn from other girls and give them the benefit of my own particular techniques to keep my slaves in their place. I find that a whole range of games including boot-worship, strap-on training and just generally trying to confuse the easily-confused male slave brain, all work well with one of my desirable female friends coming along to help me. There is something particularly demeaning and degrading for a slave when he is forced into some humiliating ritual, such as cleaning his Mistress's boots with his tongue, when that activity is demanded in front of two domes together. It also opens up all sorts of other games, such as 'spit-roasting' a man with strap-on cocks thrusting simultaneously into his rear and deep down his throat. I pride myself on training my few, very lucky, owned slaves to do whatever I may require of them. These are men who have devoted themselves to my service and who have amused me enough to become my property to hurt and abuse whenever and however I wish. 'However humiliating, however degrading' is their much-practised mantra and sometimes it is fun to be able to show off the depths of their training to an appreciative female colleague.

Many of my double-domme sessions provide an added dose of public humiliation for the most fortunate of my slaves. They are filmed for far wider exposure, both on my own websites and on various international clip-sales sites that spread my images around the world. I take a lot of care in writing and planning my film scripts to create a realistic, sexy and entertaining scenario that best shows off my own domination skills, and those of the other dommes.

The first filming session I did with another Mistress, many

years ago now, was a memorable day. I had taken my film crew to the London dungeon of 'Mistress Strap-on' who, as her name would suggest, specialised in some of the most extreme forms of anal play for her enthusiastic submissives. Waiting for us both in the dungeon, already naked and in bondage, was one of her most loyal slaves. The behind-the-scenes atmosphere on a film set is always friendly and I introduced myself to the tightly bound slave and briefly discussed the scenes we were about to produce. He was a charming man, urbane, cultured and very much looking forward to the experience. I leaned over him, chatting amicably for some minutes, as the crew busied themselves arranging camera-angles and lights, then we all switched instantly from friendly to professional. Within moments my chatty demeanour had vanished, to be replaced by my sternest voice and the filthiest insults I could muster as I castigated the wretch for some imagined misdemeanour and left him in no doubt as to what his punishment would be.

Mistress Strap-on set about living up to her name by penetrating the business end of his body with a massive rubber dildo attached to a leather harness around her waist. In the meantime I was pinching, pulling and stretching his nipples to make him moan for the camera. It was slightly surreal, tormenting this man with whom, just a minute or two earlier, I'd been passing the time of day, but that's entertainment for you. He couldn't speak to me any longer anyway because of the gag pumped up tightly between his lips. We all quickly forgot that the camera was there and had a session which we all enjoyed. Well, actually, I'm not quite so sure about our victim. In the middle of the session, Mistress Strap-on told me that her slave had a particular kink which she loved to indulge. 'He likes me to slowly insert a large dildo deep into his rear,' she said, 'and then wants me to pull it out again – as quickly as I can – like *this*.' Since she was demonstrating her technique whilst she was explaining it, her last few words were almost drowned out by an agonising scream bursting out from underneath her tied-up slave's gag. 'Oh, oops,' she announced, with a shocked look on her face. 'I've got the wrong slave; this one doesn't like that at all.'

Another Mistress and I did slightly less harm to our slaves on another recent double-domme shoot in Birmingham. I was working with one of my favourite people, the delightful Mistress Rouge, and we filmed for a whole afternoon on a purpose-designed film set which included an entire schoolroom, complete with desks, blackboards and even a separate headmaster's office to deal with the most unruly pupils. Having been at the receiving end of a few telling-offs from teachers in my time, it was a delight to turn the tables and dish out the punishments to a select group of submissive pupils. We'd dressed up a couple of the 'boys' as schoolgirls, complete with pigtail wigs and it was good to see how everybody went along with the filmed role-play, competing to be the naughtiest and therefore the first to be sent the headmistress's office for a severe caning. At the front of the class, perched slightly inelegantly on a desk, sat Mistress Rouge and I. I thought we looked the part with our long schoolteacher's gowns and tight black skirts; although perhaps we shouldn't have shown the boys and girls quite so much of our sheer-stocking-clad legs. It was almost as though we meant to tease them!

CHAPTER 26

TRUE LOVE...
AT LAST

My experience of hiring a male escort and the fun of sublime sex with him, made me realise how much I was missing real passion in my life.

I've no doubt that I excited my paid-for handsome young partner that night in the hotel bedroom – and the naughtiness of the situation and his hunky body certainly excited me. Despite my earlier doubts, I didn't have the slightest regret about what I'd chosen to do in order to relieve my sexual frustration. In fact, I had to give myself a serious talking-to in order to resist the temptation to do it all over again a few days later. I can be a greedy girl when the mood takes me.

Nevertheless, there's a world of difference between the forced passion of commercial sex and the heart-warming satisfaction that comes from making love to a much-desired, real-life partner. It is a difference I'm aware of in my day-to-day working life, fulfilling the BDSM fantasies of men, women and couples who are all seeking a form of sexual excitement that they cannot easily find elsewhere. Men profess to love me all of the time. In the throes of sexual excitement, when I have stretched and tormented and bullied their bodies into climactic submission, their emotions can run away with their minds and they'll gasp out their adoration for me. 'I love you Mistress, thank you Mistress, thank you… please hurt me again' are phrases I hear all the time. The trick is for neither them, nor me, to take it too seriously. I call it 'mind-fucking' my clients, leading them by the hand into what some term 'sub-space', a slightly altered consciousness where nothing matters for that moment other than the pleasure and excitement flooding their system. That's when they will love me… for a while. Once their lust has been satiated and their minds recover then they want to get off home to normal life and to their much-loved wives and families.

There are a few rare exceptions to the rule: the one or two men who do fall genuinely, head-over-heels in love with me and become addicted to my company, however much I hurt or mis-treat them. To be fair, I do always try to warn them when I recognise the early symptoms of Miranda-addiction.

'Be careful slave, you're going to get hurt,' I tell them. 'Keep on seeing me and I'll fuck your mind to the point where you won't be able to stop. Are you sure you want to do this?'

On the rarest of occasions I will have to nip the addiction in the bud and tell a particularly obsessed fan that my door is no longer open to his visits but, if they're not too much of a nuisance about it, then I don't mind men loving me. They're the only ones in danger: loving me can seriously damage your bank balance.

One client who I've known for well over a decade once asked me: 'What's it like to be loved by everybody you meet?'

He saw the look of surprise on my face and explained: 'Don't you understand, you are our ultimate fantasy woman because we all want to be the one who is under your guidance 24/7; in our fantasy world we all want to be the one you are with.'

I had never really thought about that to be honest. I suppose not many people spend their working day being an adored goddess, which is exactly the term he uses for me; a slightly strange thought, but not at all unpleasant. This particular slave delights in telling people that I'm his religion. In that box on government census form that demands to know your religious affiliations he writes 'Mirandite'. He is the founder, and one of very few members, of the Mirandite cult; he worships at my feet and it's no exaggeration to say that his entire life revolves around me. Despite that, I am grounded in reality; I truly am! I know that I'm just like everybody else but that I do attract men who are seeking a woman to put on a pedestal and worship. There is a fetish-magazine publisher I know who complains that some of the Mistresses he deals with get false ideas about their own status in life.

'Honestly, Miranda, some of them think their shit doesn't stink,' he jokes. 'At least you never fall for your own hype.'

With all that in mind, my own flirtation with paid-for fun and games simply made me think that it was about time that I sorted out my own, unimpressive, love-life once and for all. As you'll have realised by now, my track record with men wasn't great. I was into my thirties with two disastrous and lengthy relationships behind me, both of them with total losers. Although I'd have been too modest to say it at the time, it was clear that neither man had been remotely as intelligent as me and neither had been worldly-wise or sophisticated enough to open my eyes to all the cultural and intellectual treats that London had to offer. Even more worrying, neither of them had ever been great shakes between the sheets and each had soon lost all desire to keep me sexually satisfied. I'd devoted myself to building up my business with barely an evening off in years and both of my partners had been perfect couch potatoes. I had always wanted to live life more fully. I wanted to go into town for fun nights-out, I wanted to go out for meals and I wanted to travel. My former partners hadn't been interested in that at all. My last boyfriend had particularly firm views on the subject: 'If the telly's on and there's beer in the fridge, why would I want to go out?' He was fat and lazy and rejected any suggestion that London might be interesting: 'Why do I need to go into London? I don't want to go into London.'

Although I criticise the guys, I am aware that I'm not entirely blameless here. People have asked me why I didn't go out and do things with girlfriends. Why didn't I go out on my own to experience all that our capital city has to offer? The answer is that sometimes it was hard to give up the money. When the choice is a night out in town on your own, or earning £1000 with a client, I too often came down on the side of the cash. *Mea culpa, mea maxima culpa.* The truth is that I had nobody but myself to blame. I'd been content to lazily slip into each train-wreck of a relationship simply because that was easier than finding a suitable man. What on earth had I been thinking of? I determined that the next guy would be different. If I could recruit the perfect escort with a little effort and internet research, then surely I could find my perfect, long-term partner in just the same way?

Several weeks went by before I put my dating plan into action. Then one day I thought, 'Right, *now* is the time for me to find someone new.' But I was facing the problem that faces a lot of single women every day. Where the hell do you go looking for a man? I hardly drank at the time and the only place you would ever find me, if I wasn't at work, was in training in the gym. Even then, although I was always trying to keep my body in shape for work, that would only be for an hour each evening. It's also not the best meeting place. So where do you meet people? I honestly don't know. So I thought, 'Bugger it; I'm going to start looking on the internet.' That, of course, created a new dilemma. If I logged-on to straight internet dating sites, and was in any way honest about myself, then 'normal' men were going to think I was some kind of nutter. If on the other hand I used fetish sites and mentioned what my job was, then I'd be inundated with wanna-be slaves. I didn't quite know what to do.

The other worry was that my former boyfriend was still sleeping downstairs in my house. I think he had a vague hope that if he stuck around for long enough then we might get back together again. Now I told him in the clearest possible terms: 'I'm looking for another man, we're finished, it's all over, this is an ex-relationship. You have to go, right now. It's my house and you have to leave.' At long last he finally took my subtle hints and left. The way was clear for finding the perfect replacement. I joined a website called Alt.com which described itself as being for the BDSM alternative community and which had a dating section allowing you to put up messages seeking new friendships. I didn't mention that I was a professional dominatrix, but I did make it clear that I was very much a dominant woman, hoping to meet a submissive man.

After a few false starts, one man started writing regularly. Tony's emails were flirty and fun and he seemed to be an intelligent guy. When I saw his picture I realised he was also good-looking and had a great body. Although I was being ultra-cautious, I did slowly grow more and more interested. I began to look forward to his messages each day. We wrote to each other a lot, discussing the fetishes which had drawn us to this alternative website in the first place. I was careful to play it cool, really cool, and so after my original contact I let him do all of the chasing. He would email or text a message and I would reply – but I was never the one who instigated the next call. Soon we were sending emails backwards and forwards: he was discussing what he liked and we were creating various fantasy scenes and writing stories to titillate each other. I remember once I sent him a text message describing how I was sitting at my desk and wishing that he was kneeling on the floor in front of me. I went on to tell him precisely how I was going to bury his head between my legs and use his tongue for my pleasure. Tony's heartfelt reply made me giggle: 'I am standing in Waterstones with a hard-on. NOT good.' Actually, after months of living like a nun, that sounded pretty good to me.

TRUE LOVE... AT LAST

This was an experience I had never had before. It may have been courtship by emails and texts, rather than face-to-face contact, but for the first time in my life I was actually being wooed by a man. Previously, I'd always jumped into relationships as a matter of convenience. I'd never made men work hard to catch me; I'd fallen into their laps with little effort on their part. Now, I had a man trying hard to impress me; a man who really wanted to be with me. I can't even remember at what stage of our internet friendship I told Tony I was a professional dominatrix but I do remember that it didn't worry him at all. My new friend was open and honest with me and told me that he didn't have much experience. He said that he'd dabbled in BDSM games with a former lover but hadn't explored it as deeply as he wished. There were a lot of specific things he wanted to try. Between us we would craft elaborate scenarios and fantasies which I knew were exciting him. I was enjoying myself immensely as the emails flew back and forth, with each of us teasing the other about what would one day happen between us. By now I was sure that I wanted to meet him in person but there was to be yet a further delay. I'd recently had surgery on my knee and I thought, 'I can't arrange a meeting with this really fit guy, and then turn up hobbling around on a bad knee. I've got to be patient and wait.'

Eventually, a few weeks after Christmas, I agreed to a meeting. We both knew by then that this would end up in the bedroom and I'd already picked a local hotel. I hope you'll excuse me if this is one sexual encounter about which I don't go into all of the naughty details. This one was just too personally special to share. Suffice it to say that his body was amazing and his mind was even better. We clicked immediately and couldn't stop talking, even though we were both desperate to get to the room and start exploring those wild sexual fantasies we'd talked about for months. When we did finally end up in bed, the sex was mind-blowingly good for both of us. By the end of the night I knew two things: I wanted this man in my life… and the last thing I was going to do was let him know that.

I was pretty sure that Tony was as smitten with me as I, secretly, was with him. The number of texts and emails he sent me in the days that followed seemed to confirm that. 'I had such a great time… you're wonderful… when are we meeting again?' he asked, over and over again. Being the cruel Mistress that I am, it was easy for me to simply ignore every mention of a future meeting. Instead, I would email him back, chatting away as though nothing had happened and just being sexy and friendly and fun. 'Yes, but when are we going to meet up again,' he demanded with ever-increasing urgency. I could tell I was driving him crazy but was determined not to let him think that he'd impressed me in the way that he actually had. I did, after all, have vast experience of teasing men and keeping them strictly in their place. I kept him dangling for weeks. Finally he reached his breaking point. 'Okay,' he wrote, 'I'll leave it with you. I can see you aren't keen to meet up again, I'll leave the ball in your court.'

'Oh well,' I replied 'how about Wednesday next week?'

Even then I was being somewhat cruel to the poor guy. I knew that he worked in central London and that his job meant waking up ridiculously early on weekdays. It would have been so much easier for him to see me at the weekend, but I didn't want to make this easy. As I'd hoped, he didn't even argue: 'No problem, Wednesday it is then, definitely, definitely.'

From then onwards the relationship blossomed. We were meeting a couple of times a week and having fantastic, amazing, mind-blowing sex. I knew that I'd met someone very special. After years of living with losers, Tony was on a par with me and I was overwhelmed with sexual attraction towards him. It was so good to meet a man with a like-mind to me. The great body and the fact that he was very well hung were a bonus – most definitely a bonus. He was still working in town and, for the first time I was being taken out properly on dates and exploring the city in which I'd lived for all of my life. There was a memorable evening a few weeks into our relationship when he took me out to a top-class, Michelin-starred restaurant. It was something my former partners would never have dreamt of doing for me. I felt I was truly in a genuine relationship, being wooed in a way that all girls should be wooed. I realised how much of life I'd been missing up until then. Tony was showing me how a relationship should start, if it means to go on.

In the bedroom too, our new life together was a revelation. For the first time I felt that I was fully exploring my own sexuality, discovering pleasures that I had never experienced before. I know that probably sounds odd to your ears, because I had been sessioning for years and exploring a myriad of wonderfully kinky things in my working life. The truth was that I had been fulfilling everyone else's fantasies and dreams but never having my own fully explored or fully met. I had always got a sexual kick out of my work but never the sort of sexual excitement and enjoyment that my relationship with Tony was now providing in full. Even more importantly, I felt I had met my soulmate; not only for the support and companion-ship he was giving me but also because he was ticking all the boxes that previously had been missing from my life. Tony made me a whole person and made me very happy. We've since been together for more than five years and we now work together as well, building my businesses in a way I could never have done on my own.

Some long while after our friendship had turned into love and our lives had become inextricably intertwined, I mentioned to Tony that I missed the sexy emails and texts that he once used to send me. 'They were my wildest dreams and fantasies,' he told me. 'Why do I need fantasies anymore? I've got the real thing.'

A short while ago, Tony and I got engaged. My grand-father always said that his dearest wish was to walk me down the aisle but until I met my current partner I had no intention of doing that. I'd always thought: 'What a shame that Granddad's never going to get his wish – but marriage isn't for me.' My grandfather is long gone now of course and I miss him every day. But it may not be a bad thing that he won't be at my wedding because I have some very specific ideas as to how it might be. It will be a ceremony fit for a dominatrix princess. To hell with a virgin-white dress; everyone else can wear white. I'm planning on wearing a kinky, blue latex creation that will blow my husband's mind. In my head, my idea of marriage is dragging my man, kicking and screaming, into my cells. Then, after the slave auction is over, the half-a-dozen hunky, well-hung, 'best men' can have my full attention.

I have many flights of fancy like this – on an hourly basis. Please don't tell my fiancé!

CHAPTER 27

A STAR OF STAGE AND SCREEN

Finding my soulmate has benefitted not only my social life but also my business career. I've long had a presence on the web, but it was a bonus to discover that my partner Tony was an experienced IT consultant and could revolutionise the websites which were becoming more and more important for my company. With his help I've expanded both my private members' club site and have boosted the sales of my films across various internet platforms. Together we've opened up a whole new world of international business. Our latest venture has seen us launch a new film-clips site, hosting films that have been produced not just by my production company but by other dominatrices both here and in Europe.

I'm constantly amazed by how comfortable I feel when performing in front of the camera. At school, speaking in front of a crowd would have been anathema to me. I never wanted to be singled-out; I felt uncomfortable hearing my own voice and having others listen to me. Even reading out loud in class made me wish that the ground would open up and swallow me whole. None of that was because I couldn't read well but because others were hearing my voice. When it came to school plays I would seek out the most insignificant one-line roles, although even then my nerves would overcome me and ensure that I would fluff my one tiny line. The fact that I was so retiring is one of the reasons why my spelling remains poor to this day; I was too shy to ever draw attention to myself by even asking for help in spelling difficult words. So, how odd is it now that once the camera starts rolling I can chat away for England? Part of it is that I am usually talking about a subject dear to my heart — bondage, domination and the humiliation of my ever-willing slaves. A filming day is a fun mix of sex, naughtiness, laughter, a lot of stress and what I like to believe is organised chaos. My office, normally my haven of peace and quiet to which I can escape for a moment during a busy day of mistreating multiple clients, becomes a dressing-room, make-up salon and film crew canteen all rolled into one. Were you a fly on the wall, you would see some interesting sights.

I can often be found half-naked in the middle of an essential costume change; there may be other beautiful Mistresses or petite slavegirls in a similar state of dishabille. My cameraman will stroll through us all seeking batteries or tripods, and a trusted 'owned' slave will be satisfying my constant demand for more coffee. The doorbell will chime as volunteer slaves turn up for filming sessions, telephones will ring with new clients seeking appointments and in the dungeon outside other actors will be struggling into tight leather pants or shiny rubber body bags. It may appear at first that all is confusion, but that is not the case. I rule over my empire with a rod of iron; woe-betide those who mess up my schedule for the day. Filming is a demanding and expensive business.

Even on non-filming days my dungeon will be busy with a succession of clients arriving at regular intervals throughout the day and there's always a ton of cleaning, sterilising and tidying up to do between each appointment. Each of my rooms is thoroughly cleaned after each appointment and I will need to ensure that the correct equipment is in place, and instantly to hand, to give my next client precisely the service that he or she may require. On top of all that, my business, like any other commercial concern, runs on paperwork: invoices to be prepared, supplies to be ordered, financial records to be kept and a master diary of all of the daily activities to be maintained. Peculiarly to an adult business such as mine, the confidentiality of my clients is all-important. For that reason, my financial and tax papers record no names whatsoever. All of my clients are known to me via a series of unidentifiable code words or nicknames.

One of the major changes that my partner has helped me institute within the business has been the concept of longer-term strategic thinking. Because of the way I drifted into my work as a dominatrix, planning for the future was never a strong point. That was partly a factor of operating on the fringes of society, never quite knowing if my premises would be shut down or what the future might hold. I was also working on my own, with nobody I trusted to help focus ideas. It's just in my nature to be always full of dreams and always wanting to be busy. Many years ago a friend coined the nickname 'Whirlwind' for me. 'You've always got five things in your head at once,' he said. 'Slow down, slow down.' On the positive side, I do have some notable business strengths: I'm always on the ball with answering emails and telephone calls, I'm never late for my sessions and I'm pretty good at scheduling, not over-lapping appointments and avoiding general cock-ups. I think I've done OK.

I'm sometimes asked what advice I would give to any woman wanting to emulate me and start up as an aspiring young dominatrix. There's only one answer, which is to get yourself £50,000 in the bank first, because you'll need the equipment. There are plenty of competing Mistresses out there who seek to offer specialties such as corporal punishment, foot worship, face-sitting or whatever, and who think the only equipment they need is a cane or some thigh-boots. The problem is that men will visit them once and never return. If you aren't prepared to put in the investment to do the job properly, men soon realise you are not seriously interested in the game and will look elsewhere for those who are. My own deliciously-equipped premises have been furnished and crafted over many years. I pride myself on having equipment most men can only dream of, but I'm always seeking more. Every international film trip now has to include a visit to the local fetish equipment suppliers; I'm still a sucker for anything new.

That desire for novelty has led me to search for new and exciting film locations and for contacts in the adult film industry. I make frequent visits to various European cities –

Berlin, Frankfurt, Amsterdam, Madrid and so on – to meet and film with other dominatrices. Each girl and each location brings a flavour of the kinks of her own country and culture; I rarely return from such visits without a new idea to incorporate into my own play back in London.

One market, the biggest of them all, has proved a tougher nut to crack. Ever since I was a little girl I had always been fascinated by the sights and the sounds of America. My little girl fantasy figure of Madonna and the American life I saw on television all made me want to be there. One of the few regrets in my working life had been turning down the chance to work in California many years ago. However much I would have loved to work there, it would have been too big a leap at the time. The USA adult film market was dominated by close-knit BDSM communities and by the few major companies. My approaches to some of the major film companies had never been successful. Now I was trying again. Hollywood was calling. I had to answer that call.

CHAPTER 28

THE AMERICAN
DREAM

In the summer of 2013, just six months before the milestone of my fortieth birthday, I finally achieved a lifetime ambition to break into the toughest, the most competitive – and potentially the most lucrative – adult market in the world: the American film business.

This was not Hollywood, this was far better than that. I had arrived in San Francisco to make movies with some of the most creative and imaginative bondage experts on the West Coast of America. Ahead of me lay further film dates with one of America's most successful dommes in Pittsburgh, Pennsylvania, and filming sessions in a famous BDSM parlour in New York. As my British Airways flight touched down at San Francisco's modern and stylish international airport, I couldn't help but think how far, both emotionally and geographically, a lost little girl from a council estate in West

London, had come. From a teenage student cycling nervously through the streets to fulfil my first dominatrix appointments, to an internationally recognised performer travelling by limo in America. I'm sorry to say that it was hard for a moment not to be just a little immodest: I felt that 'The Bondage Mistress' had arrived.

My breakthrough had come by not targeting the faceless corporations which control much of the USA film world. Instead I'd concentrated on making personal contact with fellow Mistresses in the US. I wrote letter after letter to the women I genuinely admired, seeking invitations to visit and work with them on their side of the Atlantic. Over time, my persistence paid off and soon I was able to plan my first film trip in the USA. After such a lot of effort, my first night in San Francisco did not disappoint. My London-based camera crew and I were collected from the airport by a film company representative and an hour later we were admiring the astonishing studio premises of the team from the Serious Bondage production company. Tucked away in a quiet residential street to the south of the city, the company produces many of the best bondage films in America. Their two internationally-available websites cater for both fem-domme enthusiasts and, as you would expect in the gay-friendly town of San Fran, to a growing audience of same-sex bondage fans. For a self-confessed, restriction-equipment freak like me this was bondage heaven. Shrugging off the weariness of the long flight, I set off for a delicious meal of Pacific Snapper in one of the friendly restaurant bars nearby and then decided that filming could wait while I had some American fun.

THE AMERICAN DREAM

One of my favourite clients, a regular visitor to see me in London, was based just a few miles away in the pressure-cooker environment of Silicon Valley. Knowing that I was visiting the area, he had been begging for weeks for the chance to meet. It took just moments for me to call and arrange a special treat for my computer-geek friend. Within the hour he was standing naked in front of me in one of Serious Bondage's extensively-equipped playrooms. Around us on the walls was a cornucopia of chains, manacles, hoods, cages and the astonishing range of elaborate equipment that appear in the company's films. I, however, had been plotting for weeks to reduce my American slave to a submissive mind-state he had never experienced before. This particular client is extremely claustrophobic and had confessed to me months before that his greatest terror was of being buried alive: perhaps not the wisest phobia to be afflicted with in a city synonymous with earthquakes. It was a confession I had stored away for future use and had never forgotten. This night, I had decided, he was going in 'the pit'.

In the centre of a wooden patio deck built out behind the film company's studio is one of the prized possessions of the Serious Bondage crew: a concrete-lined, six-feet-long underground chamber with a heavy, foot-thick hatch that can be padlocked in place. Once shut it allows barely the tiniest chinks of light to filter through into the depths below. Still in the summer dress in which I had travelled out from London, I led my submissive onto the deck and showed him the hole. He was by now visibly shaking and begging that I should inflict any other punishment I wanted, if I would grant a reprieve from the horrors of a night underground. Just for a moment I considered taking pity on the wretch and finding another game to play. But I had waited a long time to bring this slave truly to heel and no self-respecting bondage Mistress can ever go back on her word. I enlisted the help of Dalton, my Serious Bondage host, to fit a strait-jacket in place and then ordered my victim into the pit. He was soon chained to the shackles on the wall – a necessary precaution to foil any attempt he might make to touch his cock in the hours ahead. In the end I actually had to stand on his head to force him down far enough for the hatch to be lowered and locked into place. It meant his last sight of the open evening air was a clear view of my knickers as he stared up my skirt, a little sexy gift from me as a parting reward for his submission.

Now, the more attentive of my readers will have remembered my repeated assertions that sanity and safety are always at the forefront of my mind in every bondage session. From long experience I knew that leaving anyone bound, locked-up and alone is potentially deadly; it is something I have never countenanced over the years, even when clients have begged me for long-term lonely bondage. So as I left my slave's muffled, frantic, begging pleas behind me and returned to the house, I was not truly abandoning him without the prospect of help if he needed to be freed. A hidden beauty of the pit is a night-vision camera and audio system that constantly monitors what is happening underground and provides a real-time visual and audio feed to computer screens in the building. In my somewhat jet-lagged state, I am not sure quite how long we did leave my Silicon Valley slave in his claustrophobic hell, but watching his panic build and listening to his increasingly desperate pleas for help was an amusing end to what had been a busy, busy day.

The next day my hosts had provided other American slaves for me to torment on camera, and I had the world's most kinky-friendly city in which to do it. One of the reasons for visiting San Francisco was the possibility of a level of public play not easily available in London. I am not sure that this most liberal of cities quite knew what had hit it over the following three days of Miss Miranda mayhem. Stopping the traffic on the Golden Gate Bridge, wheeling a strait-jacket bound and hooded slave along a busy road in public to a city-centre café, and riding the cable cars in full rubber-domination uniform – these were just some of the highlights of that USA trip. Day One started with me strapping my own travelling slave into a white canvas strait jacket, dressing him in fetching turquoise hospital pants and a heavy duty white canvas hood and then taking him out for a public outing to accompany me seeing the sights of San Francisco. I was not sure that even this laid-back town was ready for me in full rubber-nurse outfit wheeling my slave package across the famous Golden Gate Bridge on a luggage cart, but nobody complained. We did however have our pictures taken by a large number of locals and tourists. My shapely 'tush' (as they call an arse over there) barely covered by my mini-length, nurse's outfit, did attract a lot of honking attention from a host of American truck drivers. Oh yes… and the bridge was a great sight too.

Next stop for my wheelie slave, tied upright onto my trolley, was the Aladdin's Cave of the 'Mr S Leather' shop, one of the great bondage stores of the world. As you would expect in this gay capital of San Francisco, most of my fellow shoppers were from the leather-biking community but they accepted this humble visiting British dominatrix warmly into the heart of their USA gay world. The assistants could not have been more helpful as I showed them my gagged slave, still tied to his trolley, and explained that I was badly in need of their best and biggest strap-on cock in order to complete the next stage of his treatment and training. And oh-boy, does Mr S have a good selection of strap-ons to choose from! I was spoiled for choice as I removed my slave's blindfold so that he could appreciate the size of the dildo that was later going to stretch of posterior. I *think* he appreciated the gesture but it is never easy to be certain when he is mumbling and drooling through his canvas hood like that. Never being able to resist new devices for my teasing and tormenting games, I also had to pick up a unique double-gag that I knew would come in very handy on slave multi-days back home.

Finally it was back home to Serious Bondage for some truly serious, kinky fun with their extensive range of equipment. With the sun now dipping low on the patio deck I wanted to try out another unique feature of 'The Hole' and so I placed a slave inside with just his head – and only his head – left above ground to see the daylight fading. It is a surreal sight to see a disembodied head, seemingly detached from its owner, popping up through a head-sized hole in the middle of the patio floor. The pleading look in his eyes made me laugh so much that I almost wet myself. Well to be honest, I did wet myself in order to produce a full 'golden shower' of my special champagne, all over his face. I think the film that was shot of him trying to cope with being both scared and half-drowned with the gushing flow is a classic that my club-site members will enjoy over and over again in the years to come.

The following day my hosts encouraged me to demonstrate the pleasures and delights of mummification, a very particular specialty in the bondage lexicon. I actually used my more than willing fiancé, Tony, for this sexy mummification scene. It turned into an intense and lengthy session, with roll after roll after roll of film and packing tape being used to turn him into a tightly-bound, and very happy, guy immovably fixed and buried deep under layer after layer of plastic, all stretched tight around a body-shaped frame in the open air. As the cameras rolled to record the entire event for posterity, I slowly wrapped each limb to ensure a perfectly symmetrical start and then taped a bondage helmet in place over his face. With Tony now utterly helpless and his head tightly wrapped apart from a carefully maintained air opening, I could feel him relaxing and enjoying the experience more with every passing second. By the time I was happy with the result, the grey metal finish resembled a giant suit of armour, with an artistically created band of red around his groin like a pair of Superman pants. It was a little touch of which I was especially proud.

That first filming trip to several American cities proved a great success. I made new contacts with a range of USA film-makers and bondage models, and was soon followed by another invitation to visit Los Angeles and Hollywood itself. My partner and I did all of the usual tourist essentials, including the Hollywood Walk of Fame and the famous Muscle Beach, before getting down to the serious business of making movies. The visit was notable for my first filming sessions with one of the stars of American BDSM movies, the beautiful young masochist, Elise Graves. With her enthusiastic encouragement to really let my sadistic side loose on her body, I made Elise weep real tears of pain and sheer terror. The fiercest of clamps all over her body, endless breath control and the fact that I was laughing at her distress, all combined to send her close to the edge. I was quite proud of myself to see real fear in her eyes and real tears on her cheeks. I think what she may not have anticipated was that I was not only going to make it hard for her to breathe with a restrictive leather hood, I was also going to push some of my freshly-worn underwear under the hood to make her life even tougher. Elise loved every moment of her torment: what a thoughtful Mistress I am: too kind for my own good once again.

To balance that kindness, I determined to be a little more cruel than usual with the rest of her session. I had bought a vast number of strong white clips which attach easily to metal hooks and can therefore be strung out from the body in all sorts of fascinating and unusual ways. Batches of these clamps on the skin under her arms, on her breast and nipples and even stretching her pussy lips wide apart soon had the tears running down her face. Tightly strapped to a bondage board which I could swing at will, Elise reminded me of the old British wallpaper advert in which a man dangles helplessly, attached to a board. He couldn't have been more helpless than Elise was as I played with her clitoral hood and repeatedly took away her air. I was having the time of my life torturing this beautiful girl and soon found myself laughing as she wriggled, pulling on her own nipples and crying out of control. The more she cried, the happier she made me and soon I brought in the final straw to try and take her up to her limits. One of my American purchases was a magic wand vibrator that also delivers a sharp and painful electric shock if I push the right button. Many of my London slaves would be feeling its sting soon enough; now, however, I started stroking it across Elise's body to induce a mix of pain and sexual pleasure that brought our session to a close

Any film shoot, whether for television broadcast or for an adult movie, is an expensive and time-consuming process. Using top-of-the-range professional cameras and the most skilled production personnel is essential to ensure the correct end result of which I can be proud. For me, the technical excellence is almost as important as the erotic bondage and BDSM content, perhaps a sign of how my life has gone full circle. When I was a 19-year-old student I wanted nothing more than to build a career in the television or film world. Now that's happening to me 20 years later, from an unexpected direction, as I become the executive producer – and the onscreen star – of productions by my own video production company.

In this internet age, the television and film industries are evolving faster and faster by the day. On my last visit to Los Angeles I was involved in what I believe represents the future of the television industry throughout the world. I was the main guest on an hour-long television talk show, streamed across the web and watched by hundreds of thousands of viewers in the comfort of their own homes. From a tiny LA studio, the Extreme Restraints website transmits a series of chat shows themed around heavy bondage and BDSM play. As the cameras rolled, I discussed my sexuality, my game-playing techniques and my love of fetish and bondage equipment, with the two presenters. Then, taking advantage of the artistic and sexual freedom of the USA internet-based show, I was able to demonstrate some of my bondage tastes upon the beautiful body of a naked, and very willing, model. Because this was a web-based programme, rather than a national broadcast show, it is truly an international event. Viewers could log in and watch for free from anywhere in the world, a fact well illustrated by the number of comments I received about my performance when I returned home to London. All in all, the trip was once again an unqualified success. It's confirmed my belief that working more closely with American co-producers offers unrivalled opportunities for my own UK-based film business to expand.

In the words of one of Hollywood's most memorable characters: 'I'll be back…'

CHAPTER 29

REFLECTIONS

I've found that writing a book about oneself can be a fascinating voyage of self-discovery. I can thoroughly recommend the experience.

As I write what may be the last words of my story so far, I'm fast approaching my fortieth birthday, perhaps time for a little self-assessment of my life, my loves and my career. And yet, until now, I've never much looked back at my childhood and how it may have affected my life. A short while ago I heard a radio interview with the German-born artist Frank Auerbach who, as a child in the Second World War, lost both parents at an early age. The details of our two stories couldn't be more different, yet his words struck a chord with me. I found myself admiring a philosophy which he explained more succinctly than I could ever have done. 'I'm not given to self-analysis,' he said. 'It never strikes me as fruitful. Given this brief space between life and death, I think the thing to do is to get on with it. It's get on, or get out.'

So, given that I share his distaste of looking backwards, I'm surprised that this book has awakened so many half-forgotten memories of events which probably shaped me in ways I may never quite understand. Over time I've become thick-skinned about things which once stung me greatly. Might I have buried some memories as a psychological defence mechanism? Or am I now exaggerating the impact of events that didn't truly matter at the time? Perhaps that's a debate best left for others to judge.

The childhood memories that hurt me the most relate to the differences between life with my grandparents and the life of others in my family. There were small but distinct differences which together added up to more than the sum of their parts: many subtle slights which hardly would have been noticed by my birth-mother but which highlighted the constant divide between 'my' family and 'her' family. Without trying to sound like a poor, downtrodden, pantomime Cinders, real divisions did exist between me and my half-siblings. Many of my clothes were hand-me-downs from neighbours, and I knew that major items such as a smart new dress, or a new set of trainers, were only for Christmas. In fact, I always did rather well at Christmas because my birth-mother and other relatives would ensure I had toys – but the rest of the year was less fruitful. I had the warmth of my grand-parents' love but my room was as cold as an icewell. Perhaps affecting my day-to-day life more than anything else, my birth-mother's family and all of my friends' families had the amazing luxury of a car. My aged granddad couldn't drive. He, Nan and I could only take the bus.

Some childhood memories can hurt more than others. When I was about nine years old, not long after I had learned of my birth-mother's existence, I was hugely impressed to hear that she and her husband and her other young children had gone on holiday to Spain. To this day I can remember wondering at the amount of money it must have cost to go on an aeroplane to a foreign country. When they got back, my birth-mother came round to my house with tiny, trinket presents for my grandparents and for me. I have no idea all these years on what those present might have been but I can still recall Eileen showing off her tan to my grandmother in the kitchen. I had never been abroad and wanted to ask: 'Why didn't you take me?'

By the time I was just a little older I was already self-censoring my financial demands. On one occasion, all of the children in my class were offered the chance of a short cruise as an educational trip. I knew it wasn't for me; Nan and Granddad would never be able to afford it and so I didn't even ask. 'It's not nice for them to have to tell me they don't have that money to spare,' I thought. 'It's not right to upset them.' When my grandparents later heard that everyone but me was going on the ship they asked my birth-mother if she could help, which I instinctively knew was awkward for them to do. I think Eileen and her husband did offer the money, but by then all of the places had gone.

One last example which springs to mind now seems so trivial that I hardly dare to mention it. And yet, it was important to me at the time: 'The Tale of the Nat West Piggies'.

The pigs in question were a set of souvenir, ceramic, piggybanks given free to children who opened a savings' account. The more money you saved, the more members of the piggy family you could collect. The bank advertised the offer on television (an advertisement which I watched so often that I can still sing the tune). An aunt gave me a few pounds to open an account and collect Pig Number One of the set, a little nappy-clad piglet called 'Woody'. Other children at school were collecting not only Woody's sister Annabelle but also the more expensive figures of the Mummy and Daddy pigs. I innocently asked my nan if I could put more money in the savings account to get the next pig in line. There was the most dismissive of answers: 'Sorry Miranda, you know we don't have the money for silliness like that. Just be happy with the little baby pig that you've got; he's adorable isn't he?'

I resolved to put the piggy family out of my mind and soon enough the craze died down at school. I probably had forgotten by then that Woody still sat in glorious isolation in my bedroom cupboard. I would never have thought any more about it except that some months later I visited my birth-mother and played in my baby half-sister's warm and cosy bedroom. I could hardly believe what I saw. There, arranged in two neat rows on her bedroom window sill, sat the entire Piggy family group. She owned Woody, Annabelle, big brother Maxwell and even pig-parents, Lady Hilary and Sir Nathaniel. I went home that day with nobody having the faintest clue why I was feeling sad; I couldn't tell anyone what had hurt me. The truth is that, however silly it was, I'd been gutted by her having the entire set. The tale had a postscript many years later when I jokingly mentioned my childhood disappointment to a friend. Days later I opened a package delivered to my dungeon and found a complete Nat West Pig family, in pristine condition, carefully wrapped and given as a present.

Looking back now I can see that none of these things really mattered, but at the time they were quite crushing. It's hard once in a while not to look at family life from my perspective and question why some of the choices were made in the way they were. I truly believe my birth-mother loved me; I truly believe that she acted in the way she thought might be right. And yet her actions, her rejection of my position as her first-born child and her unwillingness to accept me into her second family, must have influenced my life in various ways. My birth-mother and I are now the closest of friends. I love her and I know she loves me. Neither of us would ever wish to hurt the other. From talking to her many times since my grandparents' passing, I know that she did what she felt to be right at the time. And how can I ever understand the position she was in? I will never be an unmarried, 16-year-old girl struggling to cope in the 1970s. I will never be able to fully appreciate the pressures she was under when that happened. Who am I to sit in judgment upon her?

All that I can try and judge is what effect nurture had over nature in shaping my life. Did childhood envy and my grand-parents' relative poverty make me more money-conscious than others might have been? Did my older-than-usual parents lack the empathy and control which might have led my teenage self along a different track? Did being homeless and thrown onto my own resources at such an early age shape the independence and the drive that has characterised my business life? Did teenage erotic adventures set my sexuality on a course that still determines my own adventurous sex life and the profession I follow to this day?

You may have your own opinions about those questions and your own opinions about my admittedly unusual lifestyle and career. Truth is, I cannot know the answers, and perhaps I shouldn't ask.

My working life brings men to my feet and offers endless excitement and fun; my filming career scratches the itch of my urge to be creative. I'm reconciled in a loving friendship with the woman I can finally call 'Mum' and, above all, my loving partner has filled in the final missing piece in the jigsaw of my particular life.

I am a happy woman. What more could anyone want?

AFTERWORD

In recent years there has been a concerted effort by many sections of the UK adult film industry and by the Government to seek ways to safeguard children from the dangers of the internet.

Even though many people reading this will correctly believe I am myself responsible for a considerable volume of internet adult material, I am also the strongest possible supporter of every effort to safeguard children from accessing such sites.

Members of my immediate family have young children of their own and, despite my profession and my hard-core film work, I would hate them to see the material I and my fellow dominatrices produce. Don't get me wrong: I have not the slightest problem with the availability of the strongest possible adult material, as long as it is only viewed *by* adults.

That stance in defence of the freedom of all grown men and women to see and hear whatever turns them on, and my distaste of the narrow-minded, often church-based opposition that attempts to stifle that freedom, does not prevent me from trying to protect children. No child under the age of 18 should be allowed to access adult content websites and I have tried to campaign among my fellow film-makers to ensure that safeguards are in place. My own film business is registered with ATVOD (the UK's regulatory authority for television and video on demand) and I've worked closely with them to ensure that nothing on websites under my control conflicts with their strict code of conduct when it comes to access by minors. The only way of viewing over-18 material on my sites is if you can pay by a safe debit card – not credit cards which even children may obtain.

I am yet to be convinced that ATVOD is the correct vehicle for this work – they are independent of government and seem to be primarily interested in collecting registration fees as a first step, rather than their far more important role of safe-guarding children. However, they are at the moment all that we in the UK have to enforce this work and I've been delighted to see them taking steps in the right direction.

The worry is that responsible producers, among whose number I count myself, are outweighed on the international internet by those who seem not to care who views the hardest of sexual material. Some of my direct competitors with UK-based operations appear to be immune to interference and make no attempt to build child-proof firewalls to protect their sites.

Only the creation of a level playing field in this fiercely

competitive area of commerce can truly bring about a situation where parents can rest easy in the knowledge that children are safe from internet harm. That's an aim I work towards every time we film and upload our most sexy material to the web.

– Miranda